D1331979

ANNIKA   RY SEAGER

junky
styling

wardrobe surgery

ANNIKA SANDERS & KERRY SEAGER

First published in Great Britain 2009
A & C Black Publishers Limited
36 Soho Square
London W1D 3QY
www.acblack.com

ISBN 978-0-7136-8833-7

Cover design by James Watson
Book design by Sally Fullam
Commissioning Editor: Susan James
Managing Editor: Sophie Page
Copy Editor: Julian Beecroft

Page 3 and 6: Stylist: Io Takemura; Photo by Syk; Hair by Tomi; Make up by Carol Brown.

This book is produced using paper that is made from wood grown in managed,
sustainable forests. It is natural, renewable and recyclable. The logging and manufacturing processes conform to the environmental regulations of the country of origin.

Printed and bound in China by C&C Offset Printing Company Ltd.,

acknowledgements

Without the following, this book detailing our decade of design would have never been possible – but please bare with us as with so many names to check comes the pressure of missing someone out!

So apologies in advance if this is the case, and here's an attempt at chronological order: Marie, Morny and Trish.

Sue Strudwick, Neil McRae, David Mollison, Keston Kennard, Nina Brooks, Emma Makepeace, Kelly Herring, Aruna Milson, Lisa Butler, Hans Rahn, Anya Wheatley, Prime crew, Stacey Tough, Paul Holroyde, Ness Sherry, Cat Cheung, Nico Holah, CJ December, Naoko, Jo Eckett and all at Brother UK, Colin Toogood, Fraser Stephenson, Megu at TimeOut Japan, Ofer and all at Truman Brewery, Andy Carpenter, Pauline Barnett, Dave Jarman, Ewen Cameron, Bungle, Paulos, Yasmin Rizvi, Alex Bittner, Goran, Jonty, Chantal, Julian, Mark, Oliver Heath, Robert Forest, Vanessa Friedman, Oliver Horton, Armand Limnander, Helen Jennings, Stephen Moynihan, Louise, Tatum and Rocky, Luz Martin, Dominic Milson, Jimmy K Tel, Duncan Bone, Helenie, Jasmia, Micheal Tough, Erica Hudge, Shorty, Sally Pink, Matthew Allen, Otto Van Busch, Reenie and Theresa, Anthony Dunn, David Holah, Leonard Hughes, Charlotte Adjchavanich, Claire Nash, Rosie Budhani, Jocelyn Whipple, Jody Williams, Chris and Emily, Aluna and My Toys Like Me, Caryn Franklin, Tamsin Blanchard, Micheal Costiff, Lisa Honey, Carolyn, Mark, Ian, Lucinda, Charlene, Nick Sze and Simon Nicklinson – the list is endless!

And of course our Junky family: David Mumford, Eric Holah, Krt Williams, Cornelius Brady, Io Takemura and Agnes Kukla. All responsible for the continued success of Junky Styling and without whom the business would not exist

Danny Mac, Choccy, Justine, Ellen, Sabine, Ellie, Manu, Isabelle, Vicky, Fran, Carla, Joey, Luella, Charmaine, Nathan, Lauren – again, too many to mention but we'd like to thank you all, staff and interns alike for your brilliant contributions to the Junky Styling history.

And to all our amazing, inspiring and stylish customers – long may we serve you.

contents

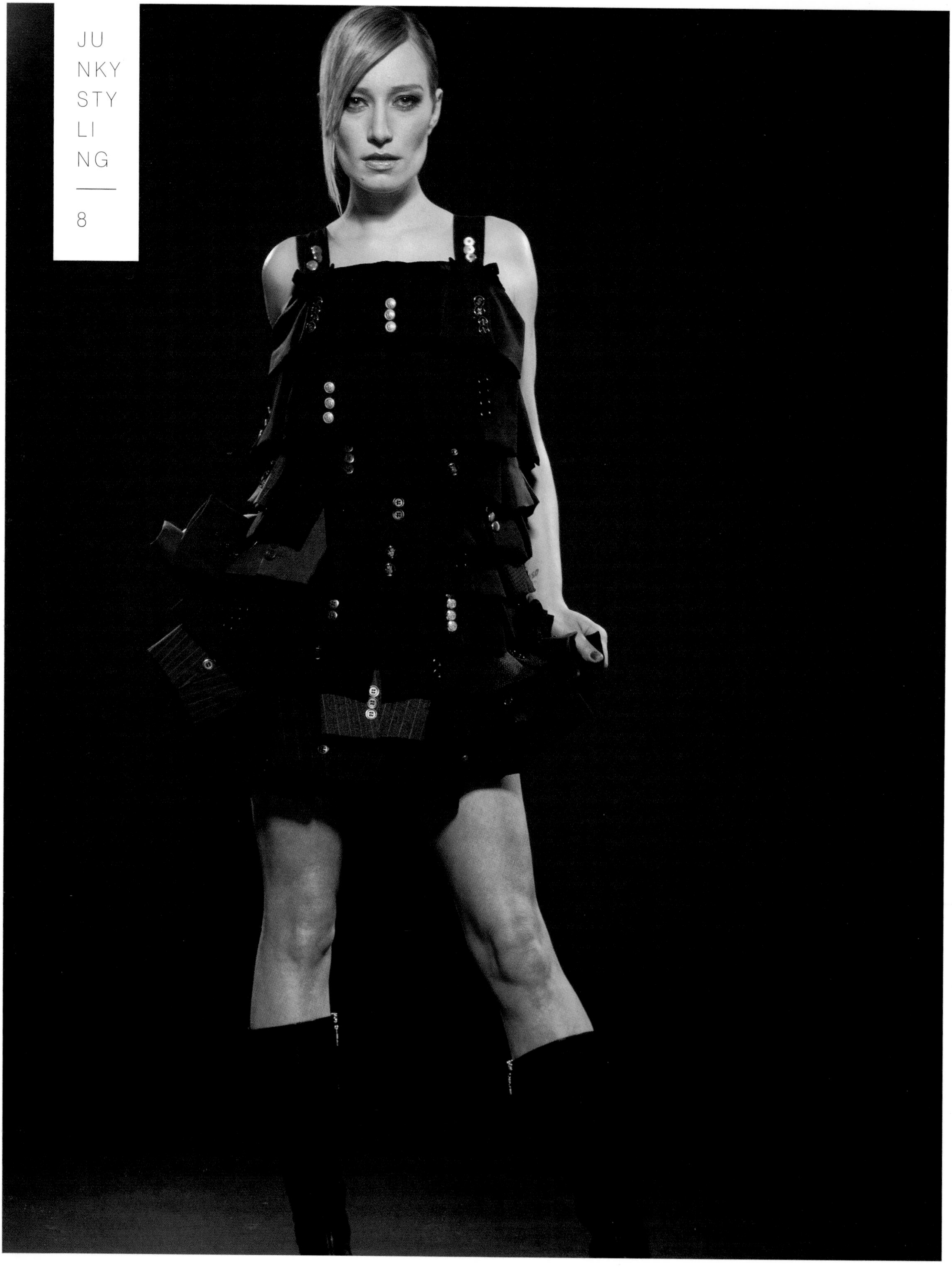

foreword

by Caryn Franklin
fashion writer and broadcaster

'm not saying we fashion types are completely environmentally unaware. Most of us and have been pushing black for years –its ecological advantages include multiple wearings and a 30-degree wash as standard – but in truth we are not as fast off the mark as we like to think.

However, now that I have experienced 'life after last season', courtesy of Junky Styling, I can boost my ethical fashion credibility effortlessly, whilst reinstating old clothes in my affections. Actually, it's a no-brainer.

I first met Kerry and her team whilst making a TV feature about ethical fashion. To put the company ethos to the test I brought in an old Paul Smith men's suit jacket. They gave it a whole new lease of life by re-cutting it into a new garment that frankly looks better on me than it ever did on the hanger gathering dust in my husband's side of the wardrobe.

Being fitted in the tiny workshop behind the main shop was like stepping back in time. Anyone watching the clothes being made on site could not fail to connect with the skills that are designing, cutting and sewing.

I was hooked after that, and I also took home a unique scarf (made from 'leftover Paul Smith') as a present to the person who had unknowingly donated the above item.

I returned to the shop, of course, and now have a beautiful party dress that was once worn by two different men! (OK, it is made out of two tailored jackets.) It gets an enormous amount of comments and interest, and, dear reader, I look marvellous in it!

Two pairs of Vivienne Westwood jeans that had languished for years in the back of the wardrobe have also been resurrected, re-cut and rejuvenated. As a result, I have a pair of very classic jeans complete with trademark orbs, star prints and original rivets that give me delicious pleasure to wear.

Now let me add another of my favourite watchwords to the mix: individuality. Nobody else in 'McFashionland' has got what I've got in

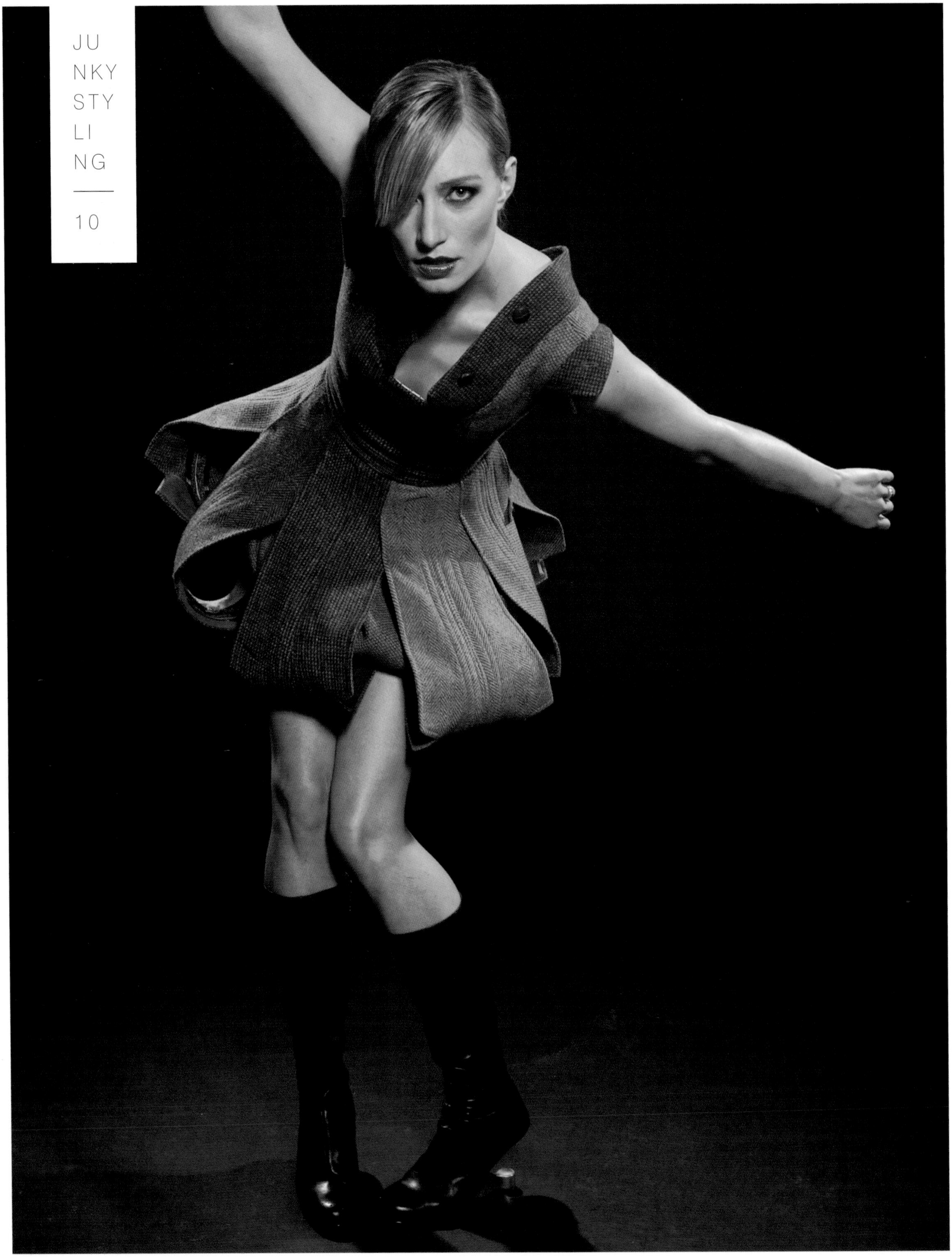

my wardrobe. My new clothes are not only recycled, they are unique.

The Junky Styling team are pathfinders, helping us to see a clever business model and a way forward that involves sustainable style.

The fact that they have been successfully trading for ten years in an industry that is notoriously indifferent to the difficulties faced by small businesses is testament not only to their abilities but also to their vision.

Ethical practice is not the new trend that mainstream fashion would have us believe – Junky Styling were doing it way back. It's just that the rest of us have taken an age to catch up.

FACING PAGES AND PREVIOUS PAGE
Erica. Photo by Ness Sherry, April 2008.

introduction

ten years of blood, sweat & tears

We jumped at the opportunity to put this book together, because the timing was perfect. Ten years have flown by since my best friend Anni and I accidentally carved out careers for ourselves in fashion. With no training in design or business and no real agenda, it has been a decade of ideas, decisions, challenges, problems, hardships and successes.

We are both a bit fast-thinking and disorganised, but we consider ourselves 'doers'. We always had an unspoken law – 'If we say it, we must do it!' – but neither of us said anything about keeping a well-documented business plan or design history; we just about manage to keep our increasing press cuttings in a file! So we embraced the challenge of sorting out our computer files, boxes of paperwork, photos and memories that chart the progression of Junky Styling over the years.

Even though the path has seen many twists and turns, I still know where to begin. I remember the initial designs and the first tentative steps into business, but the journey turned into a rollercoaster and the business has sped up, grown and diversified – so trying to explain or analyse it in these pages has been a really challenging task. Bear with us.

OPPOSITE
One of the first ever profile shots. Dressed up in 2000.

Junky Styling create timeless deconstructed, recut and completely transformed sustainable style.

sewing the seeds

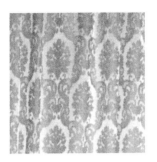

OK, so what were we thinking? Taking on a business loan and forming a partnership on the basis that we knew there must be others like us that wanted to wear a unique outfit, this was our qualification: a desire and passion both to create the clothes and to supply this niche market in our extremely unconventional way. Running a business? Bring it on.

We met at 6th-form college back in the early nineties, while studying the most random subjects, which were, unbeknownst to us at the time, completely unrelated to the life that was in store for us. The teenage years must be the most self-exploratory stage in your life. This is the time when identities are formed, and we were no different to anyone else, out and about with a whole new crew of friends, discovering new ways of life, especially the nightlife, and just enjoying each new revelation. We sucked in the energy that London has to offer, and got involved in the dance scenes particular to this amazing city alone – developing our own individual personalities, feeling special and unique within the crowd… Imagine the shock when, despite the effort put in to pursuing your own unique style, you saw someone else in a toilet queue wearing a dress identical to the one you had on, and looking so much better than you in it! Words could not describe the sense of shame, culminating in the overwhelming desire to sprint out of the club and get the night bus straight home. It was during that bus journey that I remember having the earliest inspirational chats with Anni about how this situation need never happen again.

Anni's mum had given her a sewing machine for her 18th birthday, when she had finally become sick of being resident seamstress. Working under her daughter's close instruction had all got too much, so this gift was the best possible outcome all round: we now had the tools to create the clothes ourselves and Marie Sanders had finally reclaimed her free time.

After finishing college, we both immediately got jobs to gain money to sustain our disco lifestyles. We somehow managed to save enough to grab a three-week holiday in Thailand with our other best friend Emma, and it was then that the travelling bug hit us. By now we were beginning to create bits for ourselves that we'd wear out and about to gauge reactions, but we had no idea of the impact that our designs would have as we toured round some of the major cities of the world.

In fact, it was whilst travelling in the States, Hong Kong and Tokyo that we recognised our real market. Just walking around the city streets would prompt strangers to come and compliment us on the items we were wearing. It became just the perfect research for us. It was also on this trip that we realised the importance of recycling.

In 1994, every city was doing it. I distinctly remember the impact that San Francisco had on us. The success of the thrift-store cultures, promoting individualism in the 'peace and love' environment of Haight-Ashbury.

The segregated boxes of glass, paper and tin in the basement of our apartment block – we could see that this was the right way for lives to progress. It all made sense that things should be recycled. Why shouldn't they? They'd been produced, so let's keep them alive for as long as possible. And with clothes, looking to styles of the past created a whole new feel for the wardrobe.

Our idea became clear: we would continue on our quest to make individual pieces, but for other people too. Our mission was defined: we would create unique designs from materials that already existed – stylishly. Genius.

The idea was just staring us in the face, so we knew that we needed to act fast. We knew that it was just a matter of time until many others had the same idea as us, so we sprinted back to London with our mission in mind. Now we needed money to realise our vision – and fast. But where and how?

We went to the Prince's Youth Business Trust, who taught us to create a business plan. This was an integral part of the process, as it allowed us to realise exactly what it was that we were trying to achieve, and how we could get there. When we were ready, we went up against the PYBT funding panel to see if our business idea was a tangible one. It was, and the panel agreed funding for our business partnership. That was the first of many future panel encounters. For now, we had succeeded.

We knew that we needed additional capital to open our shop and were told that we could get 'match-funded' by a bank. We were on top of the world with confidence, on a roll – until, that is, we approached the banks.

We hadn't realised that our business idea was incomprehensible to male bank managers. They saw the scene from *Gone with the Wind* where Scarlett O'Hara makes the ball gown from curtains: a pretty dress, not a business, and certainly not a business called Junky – Styling or no Styling. It was only when we met a visionary female bank manager that we were able to move forward with mission Junky, 'An Addiction to Stylish Recycling'; location: top floor, Kensington Market.

The 3 by 2-metre cupboard-size retail space was waiting for us, and we were ready for it. Lilac paintbrushes in hand, we set about building the first Junky Boutique, preparing for our first retail customer. What a buzz!

We were still creating the less-than-perfect pieces from our homes. With

**OPPOSITE Model
styled by Hennie.**

neither of us having tailoring qualifications, our main method of creation was trial and error. The finishing left a lot to be desired, yet the designs were still so innovative. Finishing is a learned skill, but design isn't, and in fact it can't always be taught.

We wanted to create, so we did, but our attitude to pricing was almost our downfall. If an item looked great from the outside but dodgy on the inside, we were loath to price it up too high, so we effectively undersold ourselves through lack of confidence, not in the styles but in the overall product itself. It made us begin to deviate from the business plan that we had drawn up, moving us away from the projected cash flows needed to keep the business viable. With the beauty of hindsight, it is clear to see that if we had had any business acumen at the time we would quickly have signed ourselves up to sewing training of some kind, but it was almost too late. There were only two of us, and one had to man the stand at Kensington Market, while the other was stitching and creating from the studio (which in reality meant either of our bedrooms). There was simply no time to learn! More importantly, we were having a great time.

It was understandable that some saw what we were doing as a hobby, and until we started taking a proper wage it probably was. It was our belief in the concept and our dogged perseverance that saw us through those early years, along with continual unconditional support from our friends and families. We were very lucky.

Kensington Market was always a bit of a dive, a massive Gothic-style building that had almost been transported into its location on the High Street. The surrounding area, W9, was pretty posh – everything that the market wasn't. We had been going there in the early nineties to buy tickets for parties whilst coveting clothes from boutiques such as Sign of The Times. The whole three floors had been painted black from ceiling to floor when the market had opened at some time in the late sixties, and by the looks of things it hadn't been retouched in all that time. To intensify the gloom, there was no natural light anywhere. By the time we became residents it had a reputation for leatherwear on the ground floor and Gothic wear in the basement. The top floor was still where it was at as far as design-led pieces were concerned, though only just, as the market's days were numbered.

It was in Kensington Market, all that time ago, that we met what is now our design team and the core of our company. Eric and David were setting up their boutique opposite us at the same time. They'd done it before about a decade earlier with the brand Nocturne; this time it was with Combination, a club-wear label specialising in latex. It was a fated meeting, and the beginning of our very long-term friendships. The experience and skill that we gained from working with them many years later when Junky Styling became

TOP Anni and Coco (our longest serving staff member).

ABOVE Our first shop sign made by good friend Neil. Kensington Market, 1997.

OPPOSITE Photo for Tendencias by Luz Martin.

a limited company is limitless. David and Eric brought with them ideas and talents, personalities and laughter. Their long-lasting friendship has given a family feel to our team that has always helped when things have been tough – and believe us when we say that there have been tough times.

Both of our stands opened on the same day, and it didn't take long till we realised the benefit of sharing staff, Coco in particular! This enabled us to produce more stock for Junky, so that we subsequently needed a larger retail space. One came up round the other side of the top floor; on the spot, we moved to the new location, and within weeks so had Eric and David!

Soon enough an even larger change beckoned. A friend of ours was part of the proposed redevelopment of Brick Lane's Old Truman Brewery. He convinced us to come and check out the space. It was amazing. It was almost all derelict in one way or another, except for the main building, which had the historical decadence of 1906, the year in which the brewery first opened. The plans for the brewery seemed surreal: to be a creative hub that would house up to 400 small businesses, including music, media and fashion. It was incredible, and we wanted to be part of it. There was a little alleyway within the Brewery called Dray Walk, which had once been where the draymen of old would come and fill their horse-drawn carts with beer to be distributed to the local pubs. The Walk was lined by twelve perfectly prepped, split-level units, and we wanted one for ourselves. The units on either end (nos 1 and 12) had windows down the sides as well as in the shopfront; coming from Kensington Market we were light-deprived. No.1

TOP Junky customers pixelated into our logo... a fusion between Fraser and David.
ABOVE Customer in shop, c. 1998. Cept148 wall piece.

OPPOSITE Kerry Fox styled by Kate.

OPPOSITE **Tie
basque and shirt
skirt, shot and styled
by Luz Martin on the
infamous green sofa.**

was directly on Brick Lane but had already been taken, so no.12 it was.

We knew that we couldn't afford to take the space on our own, but we had such a great feeling about the place that we simply had to make it happen. We needed to share the space; on that basis we'd be able to keep up two places simultaneously: one that had a stream of customers, and one that as yet didn't. Junky Styling in both East and West London – perfect. How hard could it be to find a compatible company to share the space with? Our new friends at Combination didn't fancy taking half a shop in what at that time was a derelict car park, opting eventually to move to Camden instead, so we needed to look elsewhere. We found nothing and no one. We also had no time to do a proper search for a partner, as we needed to make an immediate commitment to the place or we'd lose it. So we turned to Kieran, who'd first introduced us to the Brewery, and asked for help. He had just shown another company round the space who were in the same boat as us; they were music, we were fashion, so after a quick meeting it was decided: we would share.

seedlings

Our new address was 12 Dray Walk, the Old Truman Brewery, 91 Brick Lane, London E1 6RF. The company we moved in with was called Infant Nutrition, and a fledgling business that retailed vinyl. We used the joint initials to form the name of the store, and JIN was born with a bang of an opening party on 18 July 1998.

Ten months on and we'd moved out of Kensington Market forever and were taking over the whole of 12 Dray Walk: a split-level venue with loads of natural light, and the perfect environment for us to house the workshop and have a retail space – a true atelier. Now we were happy having everything under one roof. With sewing machines visible like an open kitchen, the manufacturing process could be viewed by anyone coming into the shop. The music vibe being kept alive with R-KIDZ selling breakbeat behind the counter, the shop became a destination.

This was our pitch to Brother when looking for product sponsorship, and luckily for us, Jo Eckett and the visionary PR department loved the idea. They provided us with three domestic machines: two straight-stitch and one overlocker. Our relationship with the company is still going strong today.

Junky Styling is a clothing label, a shop and a design team specialising in recycling clothing.

The addiction may differ, but everyone is a Junky.

junky
catwalks
&
events

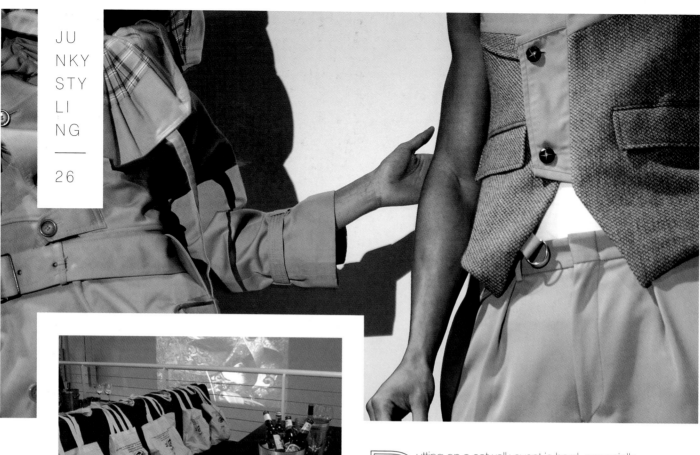

**ABOVE Eco chic goody
bags for show guests:
filled with goodies
from product sponsors
Brother, Kiehls, Shu
Uemura, Cafe Direct,
Ecover....**

**PREVIOUS PAGE
Le Parkour.
Photo by Marian Sell.**

Putting on a catwalk event is hard, especially if you do it all in-house like we always have. The process of putting together a show is a long one. Most clothing labels that exhibit on the catwalk at London Fashion Week have almost six months in which to prepare, and invariably a substantial budget that helps them outsource a lot of the work: from the press to the model castings, to the stage builders, to the sound system, to the invites, to the sponsorship, and so it goes on...There is a large amount of pressure to perform in an area such as this, and with so many chances that things can go wrong, it is a constant learning curve. We are so very lucky that in recent years we have had possibly one of the best people on our team to organise such things. Krt, who manages our shop, is a born-and-bred New Yorker and if anyone is able to get the job done, and cut through all the blagging, it is him. As the company has grown and the events have got bigger, we would not have been able to pull them off without his direction. At occasions like these, everyone needs an organiser.

The key is team and music. The music sets the mood, the team make it happen. It's hard to know what's more important, backstage or onstage. The help needed, from taping the shoes to filling the goody bags, not to mention dressing the models, which is a nightmare if they have more than two changes each ... Oh, and if you put on an event like this, don't ever expect to see it happening. We haven't viewed one of our catwalks in real time since they began.

The first show that we ever took part in was for charity. Because the event was being held locally at the Vibe Bar, we got involved. The memories of it are pretty vague, but we remember getting a good friend of ours, an amazing graffiti artist

INVITATIONS The
creativity with these
is infinite. We've used
hankerchiefs, shirt
cuffs, bookmarks
and even reused old
7-inch records.
Photo by Ness Sherry.

called Cept148 to go out on the catwalk dressed in Junky and spray some graffiti right there on the stage (health and safety was no real issue then).

The second show that we put our clothes into was for a north London modelling agency called Fluid. The event was held in a swanky members' bar in west London, called the Cobden Club, to show off how gorgeous all the models were. And they were.

The third event we took part in was in hindsight a pretty bizarre one. It was called 10 and featured ten up-and-coming designers, but the location – Whiteley's shopping centre in Bayswater – made it feel surreal, as the audience was almost accidental.

Then we began to get involved with an underground movement called Secret Rendezvous, a collaborative catwalk event organised by Mei Hui of the label Victim. Her shop and atelier was just up the road from us in Fashion Street, so we were close enough to be able to get involved. We took part in two of these events, which were held in venues within the Truman Brewery, and showed alongside other great labels that had been picked by Mei Hui. The first one was held in the Boiler House, and this being a very new experience to us we were not as happy as we could have been with our representation. The art of actually pulling together a collection on that occasion eluded us, as up to that point we had just been creating one-off pieces to sell from the shop, not designing ranges that were to be shown collectively on a catwalk. But by the time the second show happened at 93 Feet East, a club in Brick Lane, in September 2001, we were ready with a theme. The inspiration came about like this…

We had first appeared in print almost a year earlier after a random set of circumstances found us in an edition of American Vogue – fantastic! However,

CAT
WAL
KS&
EVE
NTS

———

it wasn't quite so great to read on through the magazine and see a full-page advertisement from a very prolific designer, with a beautiful model wearing a piece that looked just like it was one of ours. This guy had blatantly ripped off one of our first-ever designs, and we couldn't believe our eyes. We'd called the piece a crossover top, a style taken from a man's suit jacket that crossed over at the front. He too had called it a crossover top! We were in shock and didn't know what to feel most. We were devastated at the rudeness with which such a big-name designer could get away with this sort of plagiarism. But worse than that, we were panicked by the thought that we would be accused of plagiarising him! We did nothing but get angry and channel all our emotions into creativity, using this incident as the inspiration for our first themed collection: Ripped Off and Striped Up. Literally.

The range spoke for itself. To us, it was emotive. To the audience, it was a collection in which items could be ripped off larger pieces to form accessories, and included many different forms of stripes in each outfit. It was a perfect exercise in channelling negativity to create harmony. God help any good looking customer, friend or family member because if they could walk, we'd have them on our catwalk!

These events were Secret Rendezvous by name and by nature; publicised only by word of mouth, the audience they attracted was a truly discerning one. But I'll never forget that two days later one of our stockists came into the shop and told us that she'd seen photos from our collection Ripped Off and Striped Up on the design table of a major high-street store: now that's someone who's very good at their job!

By February 2002 we felt ready to put on our own Junky catwalk show. It was called Twisted City, a play on the fact that we twisted up suits that men would usually wear conservatively for work, and also alluding to a darker side of London. We went all out to organise it, even redesigning the classic London postcard with the Routemaster bus for our invitation, and asking as many customers as we could if they would model for us, as we believed in characters over clothes horses. Russell Brand couldn't accept fast enough, but it was after engaging the lovely Sophie at Preo PR to promote and help with the event that we secured the stand-up talents of Simon Amstell and Adam and Joe.

Another customer, Craig, was a floral designer, so he came down from Manchester to dress the catwalk; David Holah and his friend Leonard pulled the make-up together; James Rowe from Vision did the hair; the shoes were supplied through a friend at B Store, and the show itself was styled by Kelly Herring; the sound and light were provided by Stacey Tough, the seating was borrowed from Spitalfields Church just round the way; the venue was supplied gratis from Ofer and the brewery ... In other words, everyone we possibly knew was pulled into this event; they all just wanted to see it go well, and for our first attempt, it did. But even with all the favours, the show cost us a fortune, and financially it took us a while to recover. However, we had caught the bug, and almost instantly we were thinking about next season's show. What could we base it on this time?

chinese burn

SEPTEMBER '02 (S/S '03)

In a recent material haul, we'd come across a batch of vintage dressing gowns of Chinese persuasion. The writing was on the wall that this summer range would be inspired by the materials that we had in front of us, and we were able to create gorgeous pieces that once more our friends and customers could model. Only this time – genius idea – the venue and layout had changed, a change that would stick for a while. We would use the shopfront and surrounding area as our venue for the show! With Hudge providing the tunes we knew the vibe would be right, and with choreography by CJ we knew it would flow.

As the shop is split-level, it made perfect sense to section off the back bit as backstage for the models with hair and makeup, and then have them walking through to the front of the shop onto the street, where we had cordoned off a catwalk area for them to walk round, before going back in for the next change. We were lucky enough that the street in which Junky was based was private with no through traffic. So with the Truman Brewery's permission, we took over Dray Walk, which filled up with a crowd who were all happy to get a peek at the event, though with the catwalk being at pavement level, only the tall could see! That was an aspect we would address next time around.

ABOVE: All photos by Ness Sherry. Models, friends and customers getting involved in Chinese Burn – here's to Pauline and Tree.

OPPOSITE: The 'Dressing gown' dress was the essence of both the collection and the show.

armchair thriller

FEBRUARY '03 (A/W '03)

For this collection we took inspiration from a photo of Ness Sherry's that we had seen: a dishevelled paisley-covered armchair, put out to trash on a street somewhere and randomly captured by Ness. It looked fantastic and became the theme for the collection. We managed to incorporate our own version of a Chesterfield into a skirt, and took period upholstery fabric to the limits, accessorising the catwalk with vintage standard lamps and having the opening music as the theme tune from Tales of the Unexpected. I think that the difference in the styles of production between our first two shows led us to believe that we needed to meet somewhere in the middle: still wanting to stick to the shop as a venue, but wanting to elevate the models too. It was February so we needed to think of the temperature … a marquee in the street, that was it! We took the taking-over of Dray Walk to the extreme, and got a massive marquee to house the guests, which again was dressed florally by Craig, with haunting music by Mark Thatcher and sound and lights by Stacey Tough. The show was beautiful, but everyone froze. Why? We forgot the heaters.

The Armchair Thriller collection had warm sweaters and scrap-scarves. The vintage Heals fabric that Eric found inspired the colour pallet.

ABOVE: Photo by Peter Whatmore.

RIGHT: Photo by Ness Sherry.

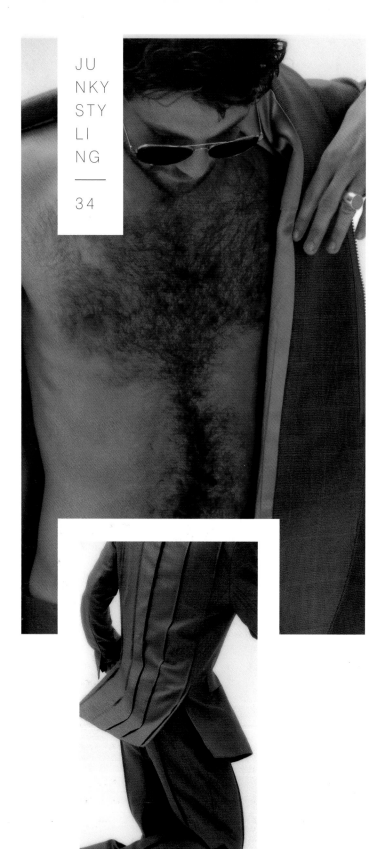

ju.st wholesale range

Anthony AKA 'Rug Man' modelled our classic structure suit and mesh bomber with joggers. All photos by Peter Whatmore. Hair by Brian.

SEPTEMBER '03 (S/S '04)

It was now that we felt ready to embark on a wholesale range for the first time ever. We hadn't yet formulated a way of recreating our recycled styles, but we wanted to get our designs out there, so we reached a harmonious compromise by sourcing dead stock (as opposed to recycled fabric) from a factory in Huddersfield – beautiful lengths of pinstripe excess which we used to create our range. The designs were comprised of winning styles that had been created for our previous show, Armchair Thriller. We took the Ju from Junky and St from Styling to establish a brand called Ju.St – the wholesale offer from Junky. We invested our mini budget in a trade show as opposed to a catwalk event, and created our first-ever brochure.

LEFT: Our friend Nina Brooks models every collection.

BELOW: DJ Hudge always serves the best show tunes and brought along 'Shorty' his 7-piece hip hop band for a live PA.

shop hop

FEBRUARY '04 (A/W '04)

We missed not having an event that September, so in February we looked to have both a catwalk in-store as well as participating in another trade show. Again the use of deadstock fabric prevailed as an alternative to truly recycled pieces in an attempt to truly create a flowing-looking range. This time the mainstay of cloth was a charcoal chalkstripe, continuing with the Ju.St manufactured range. It was a freezing and damp evening, yet the clothes were somehow sexy and warm.

We nearly had an accident when one of the models almost slipped and fell on the trunk that we had placed outside to act as an improvised podium – but I suppose it all added to the occasion!

This was the collection that we took for the first time ever to Milan, to a tradeshow called White – an amazing show that created a lot of interest in our brand, but unfortunately not many sales. It transpired that our designs were adored, but our production costs were too high to translate effectively into a wholesale range. In the light of this news, we would reassess.

don't
waste it

SEPTEMBER '04 (S/S 05)

We recycle, yes we do! We thought, 'Let's fuse our pattern pieces with our freestyle pieces and see what happens on the runway. Let's not waste any of the skills, and see what happens.' The result looked wicked! Shirts, suits, tees mixed up with shirtings, ties and denim – it was a real example of what the Junky team could create. It worked.

With the clothes modelled once more by a mixture of models, customers, friends and local faces, the show was a great fusion of Junky meets – Ju.St both on the catwalk and at the after-party. An excellent night all round, and a confirmation that we could continue to keep our ethos real – not wasting any materials with the potential to be transformed into gorgeousness.

OPPOSITE: Leigh took a break from filming 'Queer Eye for a Straight Guy' to model and is captured here by Luz Martin.
INSET: Resident model Helenie, photo by Duncan Bone.
THIS PAGE: Emma and Anthony doing their thing. Photo by Duncan Bone.

TOP: Michael, Sally, Jules and Lulu, Anthony, Oliver, Davide, Russell, Justine and Co.

ABOVE: Anni and Kerry toasting the show 'backstage'.
Photo by Duncan Bone.

LEFT: The message is clear: Recycle, recycle, recycle!

fashion loves u

FEBRUARY '05 (A/W '05)

To coincide with the bird-flu epidemic and a particularly evil winter in which everyone got ill, Fashion Loves U became the abbreviated title of our February show. Thermals were the show's customised necessity, while face masks adorned all the models. Jumpers had been cut and fused together to form dresses and tops, while jumper sleeves were sewn together to create either hoods or face/identity protectors, and suit jackets were cut up to form both skirts and basques. It was also at this show that we first experimented with boning with David and Eric's expertise.

TOP, CLOCKWISE FROM LEFT: Benoir, Russell, Helenie. Photos by Duncan Bone.

BELOW: David amongst the models. Photo by Luz Martin.

cabriolet

SEPTEMBER '05
(S/S '06)

We had always wanted our pieces to be open to interpretation, so we thought we'd take it that one step further with Cabriolet. Convertible clothes was where it was at, so we played with the idea that one design could be worn in different ways and tried to make as many skirts as we could think of that could also be tops or dresses. One of my favourite pieces from that collection was the white dress that looked almost armadillo-like, with the torso section created from very old detachable collars that were so heavily starched they stood up on their own.

OPPOSITE Linda, Laura and Sherine. Photos by Ness Sherry.

CAT
WAL
KS&
EVE
NTS

—

CLOCKWISE FROM LEFT:
Ellen and Anni at work.
On display: Using all types
of materials – even shoes!
Eric sewing.
Anni and Kerry at work.

live Installation

FEBRUARY '06 (A/W '06)

This event spanned three days of direct action, but took three weeks of material collation. We approached a local business that had an amazing space and window at street level, with the pitch that we wanted to live and create in the space. The business, a design agency called Wieden Kennedy and a gorgeous guy called Tony D, fell in love with the idea to such an extent that they called on all their employees to donate an item of clothing towards the project. By the time we were ready to begin work, the material pile consisted of everything from blankets to shoes – perfect for the challenge. Our team wheeled our Brother industrial machines round the corner to the space and began creating an amazing patchwork dress live in the window, even using the shoes to become a corset.

As well as being great fun, it was also the warmest February event that we have ever held!

three junky habits

SEPTEMBER '06 (S/S '07)

Our inspiration for this show came from my brother's wedding in a Polish Catholic church. The priest's outfit was incredible, the bling positioned in just the right places. We loved both the priest and his outfit, so we began playing with our signature suits to create our own version of the traditional dress. We pulled in an amazing set designer called Miyo, who successfully transformed the outside of our shop into a rich theatre-like setting in which kilts became amazing dress and suit jackets, and rain Macs became capes. Calling it Junky Habits was again a play on words, referring to the addictions that most of us have to some kind of pleasure or thrill, especially to Junky September catwalk events held in the street!

On the streets with the catwalk outside the shop. Photos by Luz Martin.

CAT
WAL
KS&
EVE
NTS

43

off piste

FEBRUARY '07 (A/W '07)

We'd taken up snowboarding, and went for the New Year to France. Being above the clouds and breathing the opaque air, we knew that our A/W range for that year would be based on the snow! We transformed the shop into an alpine chalet, serving drinks of hot organic chocolate laced with rum, while conducting a photoshoot in full view of our audience, showcasing reworked skiwear from the mid-eighties to perhaps mid-nineties, a time before fabric technology had really kicked in. A live performance from electro duo HeavensGate added to the event with music by Hudge and Jimmy Ktel. Recycling salopettes was great fun, and mixing them with more wearable materials such as denim ensued within a week. Note to self: Don't ever try again to recreate a snow storm with biodegradable packing pieces – they disintegrate into the floor when touched by liquid, and take hours, even days, to remove!

FACING PAGES: All photos by
Duncan Bone.

community

CLOCKWISE FROM LEFT:
The Junky retrospective
show 'Community' and
'Green is the New Black'
launch.

SEPTEMBER '07 (S/S '08)

We couldn't believe it ourselves but we were about to celebrate our 10-year anniversary in the same premises – the community that was the Old Truman Brewery – and we wanted to have a party! The area in which we had traded for most of our business lives was like our home, so we wanted to include everyone we could in the celebration. With the help of our key supporters, Brother and Kiehl's, we were able to put on a really amazing event, our biggest yet, housing almost 800 guests.

The street just wasn't going to be big enough for such an undertaking, so we recruited Jim at Swim to dress the massive warehouse space that we had been given by the landlord. We used the event as a Junky retrospective, featuring some of our favourite and most successful designs from the previous decade alongside our incredible new pieces. We'd never enlisted the help of a stylist before, but could never have lived through this event without the help and vision of good friend and amazing designer David Holah (of eighties Bodymap fame), who managed through sheer sexiness (!) to create about 60 outfits from our pieces. There were so many outfits in this show, it was truly impossible to choose a favourite. Choreographed by Carolyn at Nevs and using her gorgeous models, with sunglasses by Oliver Goldsmith and shoes by Terra Plana, United Nude and Beyond Skin, our models were beautiful from head to toe.

Our show also coincided with the launch of *Green is the New Black*, the first book of its genre to be published, written by Tamsin Blanchard. Junky were very happy to be able to play host for this event, as it really tied in with the whole ethical community feel.

show off

FEBRUARY '08 (A/W '08)

Twentieth Century Frocks was an idea David had thought of, that had been with us since we had entered the new millennium. We felt that after the success of our mass birthday event, we should look to go more intimate(!) so a new decadent venue called the Brick House had opened, and we felt that it would be the perfect place to hold a Parisian style couture event that featured bespoke dresses. We created from as varied a selection of materials as possible: shirt collars, suit cuffs, zips, army jumpers, ties, leather jackets, T-shirts, dress shirts – you name it, the team created it.

Dresses for the ladies, men's suits to correspond with them like the perfect accessories! For the first time ever we did two runs of the same show. A combination of 250 capacity and the fact that Britain's Next Top Model contestants were taking part made it happen – it was chaos but amazing. Seeing the show again on TV the following June was great, and inspired us for the next collection!

FACING PAGES: Junky 'Show off' at the Brick House with Nevs and Britain's Next Top Models. Eric's zip creations with Anni's shirt ruffles. Photos by Luz Martin and Ness Sherry.

backstage

The perfection required behind the scenes of the show is immense, and it is the people backstage that make the show happen on the catwalk. From ensuring the models have the right hair, make-up, outfits on, shoes, accessories and attitude even!

Then making sure that they know their running order, who their dressers are…. It's relentless and can be pretty stressful, so a great team behind the scenes is more than necessary, and we are lucky to have locked down the integral components.

David, Eric, myself and Anni dealing with the overview, having designated jobs but liasing throughout. David Holah being the stylist and a key factor in the makeup, with Shu Uemura and Leonard executing the look. Carolyn at Nevs being the choreographer and helping to work out the running orders. Anthony Dunn heading up the hair looks, always with amazing help. Dressers are so necessary and we are lucky to have members of the Junky Team, Cornelius and Io overseeing other helpers in the form of work experience students, past or present, so always a big thankyou to them, as aside from just dressing, they are responsible for all models eating, drinking and their shoes being taped!

ABOVE: Marie, Sally Pink and Jules. Dan Sicks, Sherine and model collective. Photos by Luz Martin.
FAR LEFT: Jules and Lulu, Oliver Heath and Russell Brand.
RIGHT: David Holath and Leonard Hughes working backstage.
RIGHT INSET: David, Anni and model.

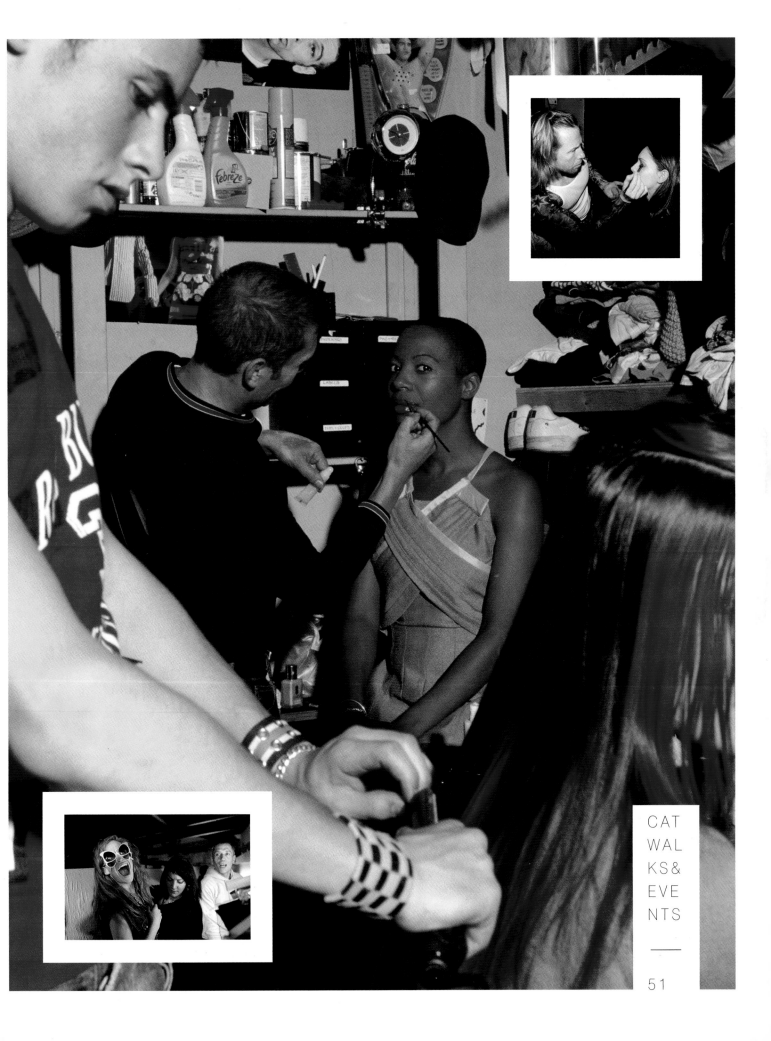

ABOVE: Jasmia.

TOP: Coco dressing.

RIGHT: Kerry helping Aluna from 'My Toys Like Me' with her skirt.

LEFT: David Holah doing Emma's make up, Anthony Dunn doing hair and Eric Holah dressing. Photos by Luz Martin.

JUN
KY
AT
LAR
GE

53

junky at large

tv appearances

Over the years, the concept of wardrobe surgery has continually appealed to the television crews. It seems the 'before and after' aspect is very attractive. Listed below are some of the most memorable appearances. Our first namecheck on TV was on Channel 4's Big Breakfast in December 2001, after a stylist had borrowed a couple of pieces that were then used on the show.

But it was Raw TV, the first ever UK digital TV station, that in 1999 premiered our wardrobe-surgery concept live on air as we reworked one of the presenter's suit jackets in the studios using a domestic sewing machine. It was a very funny day. It was so disorganised, we spent the whole time laughing constantly through a combination of nerves and genuine funniness. Anni and I had been approached to take part in the show via the shop – we were glad to be involved just for the experience it gave us, as I doubt that many people will have seen it! Somehow we managed to transform this piece of clothing while the programme was actually running – who needs a 'Here's one we made earlier' punchline!

In 2004, however, the British version of *Queer Eye for the Straight Guy* did the whole thing substantially better. First, they brought the guy whose clothes we were reworking to meet us, so that we could get an idea of who he was. Then in the same programme they had him wearing all his favourite new threads as part of his makeover; what's more, he chose Junky over Mulberry, so we were very pleased about that!

Another programme that sticks in our mind is the German version of MTV, known as Viva, on which we featured in 2005. This gorgeous female presenter was being filmed in the shop trying on all the clothes and looking simply beautiful. The obligatory part then followed with an interview with one of us. This time I (Kerry) drew the short straw and, next thing I knew, there we were, chatting on the stairs about the Junky brand. We always hope to get copies of any TV appearances that we are involved in, but when we received the copy of this particular footage and all of the team gathered round the computer to watch, what came out of my mouth was dubbed over in fluent German!

The summer of 2006 led us into a programme/market that we would possibly never have got involved in if it hadn't been for an amazing director that talked us into it: the daytime TV royalty who are Richard and Judy. As much fun as we had making the clip, and as lovely as the lady was that we made over, we soon realised that the wardrobe-surgery concept that was our brainchild shouldn't become a staple of this kind of television – it was almost too precious to be used in the new genre of makeover TV, to the extent that we didn't want to be part of it. However, the response was incredible:

PREVIOUS PAGE
Le Parkour. Photo by
Marian Sell.

OPPOSITE Jasmia
in Junky Dress Shirt
Braces and Cuffs from
our first Accessories
shoot. Photo by
Stefan Suess.

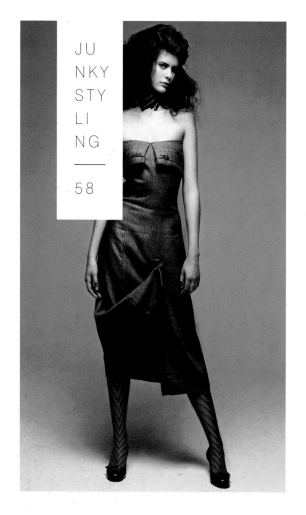

who knows how many people watched that programme!

So after dabbling with a couple more international TV programmes that year, we busted into 2007 with more of a focus. We loved the idea of being VJs so when asked by MTV Flux to present our favourite music in a green issue for the UK, we jumped at it.

This went, too, for the launch of Al Gore's Current TV in the UK. We were asked to be part of one of the short films that the station is famous for, and we really enjoyed reworking some of the LA-based presenter's bits for him to wear when he went out on the town in London.

This then set us on a roll, and by the time 2007 was finished, we'd performed wardrobe surgery for Caryn Franklin on *The Clothes Show* and Pamela Flood on *Off The Rails*.

By the time 2008 had begun, we realised just how consuming filming was, and decided to try and draw a line under it after the February 08 show. So we took part in *Britain's Next Top Model*, where the aspiring models were actually part of our A/W 08 catwalk show. It was at this time, too, that we filmed for BBC1's *The One Show* and BBC2's *Mary Queen of Shops*.

tv treatments aplenty

The pitches we've received through the years have been a great source of amusement. Once we have got past the fact that we'd never be able to, or want to, host a 12-part show so would they please stop asking us, we have been able to see the funny side.

The genres have varied a little. For instance, Charity Shop Challenge in 2000 was the first-ever pitch. It involved us driving around the UK in a Routemaster bus filled with sewing machines, finding locals and dressing them amazingly for under a fiver.

On another occasion we were asked to be part of a panel on a green forum, sitting alongside politicians and true academics, to discuss green issues on a daytime current-affairs programme. As sector specialists, we were expected to speak with authority on a variety of issues.

Most of the pitches have involved 'Richard and Judy'-style makeover treatments, with each production team thinking that their idea was the most innovative. Yet all of them wanted to project us and the nature of the way we recycle in an almost stigmatised way, by equating the skill heavily with the price. None of them were inspirational enough for us as a brand to want to get involved. As a result, we decided to formulate our own idea for a television series. Watch this space, as it should be coming to a small screen near you soon.

ABOVE Image styled by Henny: the result of a trade off for loaning clothes for a test shoot.

OPPOSITE Coco, Anni and model posing for Luz Martin shoot in the shop, for Spanish paper El Periodico.

projects & opportunities

SLAMMERS OF LONDON, UNIFORM GIG, '04

Our first range of Junky work wear involved a company of promotional girls and guys, for whom we designed uniforms to wear while out and about in London, invariably slamming tequila shots in clubs.

RELIGION

We met the owner of the brand and the head designer in our shop. They liked our winter wear and asked if we'd be able to help create some bits for them too. As they are such a massive company, with many collections every year, we were happy to be a tiny part of it. So we designed items for their winter collections, an arrangement that is still ongoing.

BELOW 'Vanity' customised Vans for Teenage Cancer Trust.

OPPOSITE 'Slammers of London' uniforms commissioned by Renata for her girls. Leg cuffs designed and created to disguise varying shoes; wrap skirts to fit varying hips and stretch back waistcoats to fit varying chests!

EXPO BARCELONA 2000

We were approached, via the shop, by an Italian stylist who'd fallen in love with a particular tailcoat that we were producing at the time. She was working on a project for Expo 2000, and asked us to create an amazing design, based on that tailcoat, for a German performance artist who was taking part in her project.

PUMA APPAREL

There was an exhibition going on near the shop, showing a collection of Puma States trainers that had been created from used textiles. Checked shirts were the mainstay of the shoes, and of course we loved them, with their ethos being similar to our own.

One of the Puma guys from the US walked into our shop, purchased some pieces for his wife and asked us if we'd be interested in working with some old stock that he had knocking around his office. We loved the idea, and as soon as the box of clothing had arrived, we got to work on recycling the obsolete stock. We were so happy with the results that we shot it instantly and emailed the images across to him. He loved them too, but destiny decreed that he was due never to touch them: we sent him the reworked bits, but the box disappeared en route, never to be seen or heard of again. At least we still have the memories.

ISTANBUL '07

An amazing Ph.D. student from Sweden had the brilliant idea of curating an exhibition called Hackers and Heretics in Istanbul. Using several designers with a sustainable ethos from all over the world, he managed to create a six-week forum of style and ideas that was easily accessible to the residents of Istanbul. We were the UK offering in this event, and our whole team – the two of us, plus Eric and David – went over there and provided wardrobe surgery workshops in the gallery for a couple of days. It was brilliant.

FACING PAGES Adam and Tree model for the Puma project in the derelict space opposite our shop. Photos by Ness Sherry.

STOCKHOLM '07

Being a part of the collaborative that is London's East End Designers, we had the opportunity to be part of a tie-in with PUB, a historical department store in the heart of Stockholm. The whole of the top floor was being revamped, its displays curated by the stylish Swedish lead singer of the Cardigans. The sector that we were part of, called Made in London, enabled some ten London brands to sell a wholesale range in the store. We were lucky enough to go to Sweden for the launch.

CLOTHES SHOW '07

This was almost a prerequisite for our launch into TopShop. We needed the opportunity to test a different, younger market to the one that we already had, and this sales event was perfect. To date, our clothes had been seen as pretty high end, due to the nature of the way they are produced, and we knew that it was limiting our market in two ways: in terms of price and availability. We needed to change tack, and develop a varied line every other successful brand has done in the last ten years. We formulated a range that was less heavy with detail, and went to Birmingham NEC to sell it.

THE OLD VIC THEATRE '08 – BRANDED

We were offered an opportunity to work with the Old Vic Theatre on a production that needed costumes. *Branded* was no average play, having been created in a fairly unconventional way. Ideas had been gathered from local schools as to what they as an audience would like to see in a performance. These ideas were then put to a playwright, who sifted through them and created a storyline with a script. Just as the production was for the kids' benefit and would be played by them, so we felt that they should also be the ones who design and create the costumes. So, with the help of the teachers and facilities at the community college in Hackney, we were able to guide the students through the process of recycling the outfits to each actor's size and specifications. The whole project was overseen by Krt, who did an amazing job.

OXFAM

The wonderful idea of rebranding some of the most important Oxfam stores into sustainable and stylish boutiques came from Jane Sheperdson, the lady who made TopShop what it is today. We were delighted to be part of this great project, which involved us in upgrading the three key stores in London's Westbourne Grove, Chiswick and King's Road.

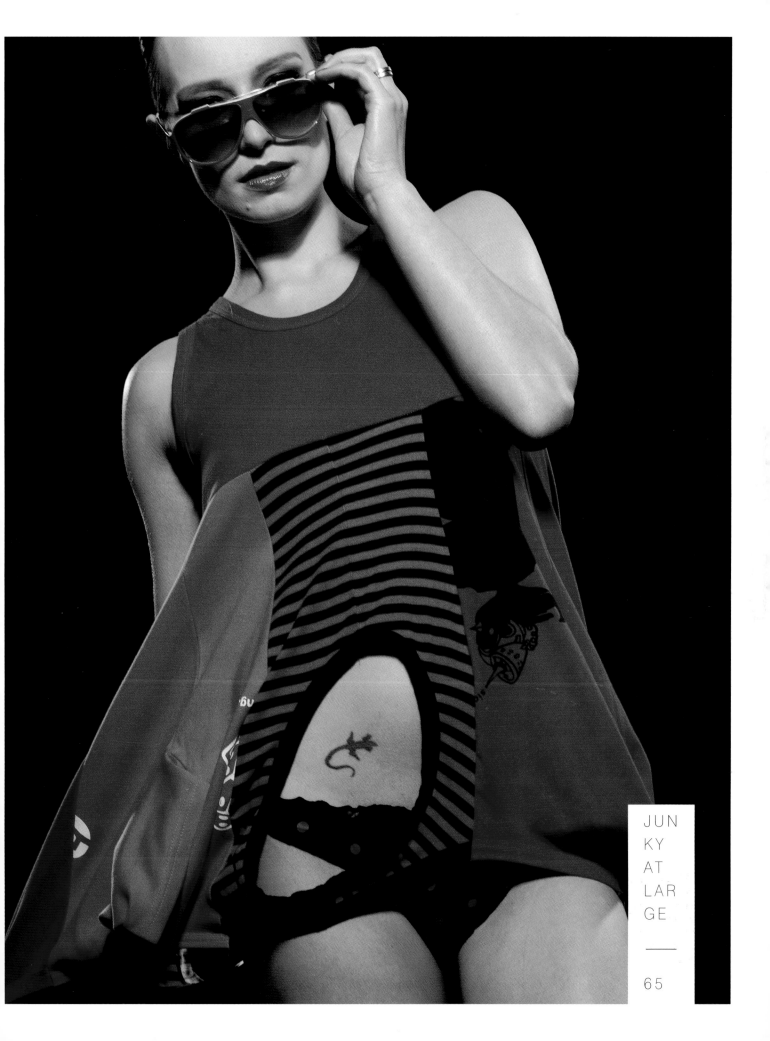

TOPSHOP FLAGSHIP STORE – BAZAAR

In April 08 we finally began selling in the TopShop store in Oxford Street. It had been a long time coming, and, having tested the market at the Clothes Show event five months previously, we felt we were ready to start selling the newly diverse range in the basement of the store, which was always our favourite floor. The importance of being able to sell our brand in there is phenomenal. The exposure that a store like this gives to brands like ours is tremendously valuable; we especially like the fact that the Bazaar section is based on design, so our ethics are an added bonus rather than a niche theme.

luck

There were many times that we felt having a shop might be a bit of an albatross, being stuck in one location and tied down with overheads and what have you, but in fact that shop of ours has presented us with many opportunities; some of them, admittedly, we weren't always able or savvy enough to take, but they were great opportunities nevertheless.

For instance, several things flowed from the recommendation of Robert Forrest, an extremely well-connected man within the fashion world. Unbeknown to us, a visit to our store in Brick Lane had struck a chord with him; so much so that some time later, while in Paris watching a John Galliano show that included a lot of reconstructed designs, he thought of us. On the strength of his observations to his friends, one of whom happened to be the features editor of American Vogue, in the year 2000 we managed to obtain press coverage from the *Financial Times* and *American Vogue*, and even got an appointment with Julie Gilhart, one of the visionary buyers at Barneys, America's finest store.

What an incredible experience it all was at the time – flying to New York, feeling special. The problem we had, though, was that we just weren't

**Other books featuring
Junky Styling**

Over the past decade our ethos
and shop space have led to
us being included in several
publications. Here are some:

Fashioning Fabrics by Sandy Black

Ultimate Shop Design by Tenues

Cool Shops London by Tenues

Green is the New Black
by Tamsin Blanchard

Eco Chic – Fashion Paradox
by Sandy Black

Eyes Open London by Ideo

Pimp London: The Guide by
Briony Quested

*Sustainable Fashion and
Textiles* by Kate Fletcher

Green Designed Fashion by
Christine Anna Bierhals

**OPPOSITE Helenie
models a summer shirt
dress, one of Eric's
shearing masterpieces.
Photo by Ness Sherry.**

ready. It was only the two of us producing the brand, and though our
ideas had got our clothes through the door at Barneys, we knew that our
production methods would not keep them there, as at the time we were not
set up to service any kind of demand other than our own.

A great stylist called Paulos was another who tried to show us the way.
He was extremely successful in styling music groups and just beautiful
people in general, and he tried to introduce us to the idea of recreating
styles that we'd already developed, to cut patterns of Junky pieces that he
loved so that they could be recreated in colours of his own choice!

The combination of not having the skills at that time, 1999, to create
patterns, and our conviction that there should not be two identical Junky
pieces, kept us on the organically growing snail trail to success, and kept
us away from the kind of fast-tracking that, with such limited experience,
could well have blown us out the water.

The shop used to close on a Monday: with the Sundays always being
such busy days in that area, we needed a day off! But the fact that the
shop was closed didn't mean that we weren't there; invariably we could be
seen through the windows, working out the back to produce stock for the
week to come.

It was on one of these Mondays that we got a knock on the shop door
from a lone stylist wanting to know if it was all right to bring 'Gwen' in; at the
time we didn't know that he was referring to style icon Gwen Stefani, who
happened to be in London and wanted to do some shopping! Two hours
and five purchases later, they left happy after getting on-the-spot alteration
services, custom-fitted to Gwen's body. We were happy, too, as this was
the closest we'd been to such a stylish lady who was in the public eye.

One of the earliest shows of interest in our label as a wholesale brand
came from Greece. Peter and his buying assistant would come to London
every season to buy British brands for their six-storey store in Athens. It
took a while to lock down the account, but once it commenced, we were
able to create a following within the city. It subsequently became one of
our longest-standing wholesale accounts, along with YSH, the boutique in
Tokyo which houses London-based labels.

Another key area in which the shop helped the brand was in product
sponsorship. Our first deal was with the sewing-machine manufacturers
Brother. They believed in the essence of Junky and agreed to support the
company with the product from the moment we began in Brick Lane. They
have been by our side ever since, providing us with machinery through
every step up in growth.

The other company that has supported us through product and
sponsorship is Shu Uemura, the amazing Japanese make-up brand. We

were very lucky to meet with the PR girl, Charlotte, who along with her team really believed in the Junky ethos. When her company began to look after Kiehl's, the great American brand, we were doubly supported at every fashion show, shoot and event with products for goody bags, makeup and hair teams, and just support in general.

photography

We hope you are enjoying the images in this retrospective. It is so important to have a rapport with the photographers you work with, as the essence of photography is to capture a moment in time, which in itself can lead to a deep-filled moment of stress for all involved if things don't go right, or there is a conflict of visions on a shoot. So we have been very lucky to be able to include some of our favourite photographers', and friends', work in this book.

Ness Sherry began her career when we did; we met in our space at Kensington Market. She did our first-ever shoot, and we've never looked back since. Luz Martin landed in our shop from Spain almost eight years ago, and saw the potential to create amazing shoots with the help of our clothes, some of which you can see here. With Luz as with Ness, it is hard to keep in proper touch, but happily our paths keep crossing both professionally and personally. Our other favoured photographer is Duncan Bone.

websites

We are on our third. When we first began the business, they weren't so prevalent. Our first site was created for us by a lovely girl called Gisele. She was on a web-build course, and approached us to ask if she could create one for Junky. What she did was great, if not slightly redundant by today's standards, being more a window for the brand than anything else. Being a design label that is ever-changing, however, we needed to try and stay fresh, so it wasn't long before we employed the skills of PYKY to create us a new site that with the ever-growing technology was now in Flash: things moved when you rolled the mouse over them – genius! Of course, this too had a lifespan, as it could not be updated in that format. So, eventually, we changed to our third and final website, which we are now able to update daily if we so desire, thanks to the help of a very talented man called Niall. The address is www.junkystyling.co.uk.

The world of retailing and the way people shop has changed dramatically in recent years. Busy lifestyles and globalisation have meant that people now need to have the option to shop from home, and Junky is a part of that revolution with our 'In Store Now' page on the site. The future for us and all other companies is the Web, and thus it is extremely important to have as much of a presence online as possible, whether this is through websites or the online communities that are growing up every month.

ABOVE Front cover of Drapers Supplement, a Metro double page spread.

OPPOSITE An amazing image from a German magazine, styled by Oliver Rahn.

press pieces

Press coverage inspires you to keep doing what you're doing; it gives you that extra boost as a team when you see something positive on paper. It can also get your name out to a market that beforehand had not known of your existence.

Our first piece of press came in 2000, written by Vanessa Friedman for the *Financial Times*, an amazing endorsement that we'll never forget. Armand Limnander for *American Vogue* put us in a recycling piece alongside Martin Marghiela, with a big picture of an outfit that we'd sent over for the shoot. The clothes looked amazing in print, our first sighting, and in Vogue, too.

Oliver Horton is a freelance journalist who has written for a lot of publications. We were lucky enough to convince him that our brand was worthy of mention, so he subsequently got Junky published in *Sleazenation* and the fashion-forecasting website-cum-bible for trends, WGSN, to name but two.

One of the most amazing images of our clothes that we have seen in print was when Amechi from Flux borrowed an outfit from our Twisted City collection and shot it against a chaise longue and flock wallpaper. It filled a full page of the magazine. Bel Jacobs has always been an integral part of London's fashion press. Her contributions to both the *Metro* and *Time Out*, amongst others, have been a constant of London's cultural life. We were very fortunate when meeting her that she chose to write about us.

fashionSPOTS

WAIST COAT: Junky
WOODEN NECKLACE
USED AS BRACELET: Made Green
CONKER: Made
BUTTERFLY MOTIF NECKLACE: Made
EARRING: Kirsty Kirkpatrick
BOOTS: Tertti

MARCH 08 39

**OPPOSITE Styled
by Io Takemura. Hair
by Helene Eriksson.
Make up by Polly
Colville. Photo by
Alex Leonhardt.**

exhibitions

We have taken part in a few of these, notably the Crafts Council exhibition called Refashioned. A touring show that travelled the length and breadth of the UK, it was seen by a lot of people. We've exhibited in Newcastle with ReDesign, a collective that puts on sustainable exhibitions, and we've also had our work in galleries in Paris, Vienna and Athens, and a touring British Council exhibition in China too.

education

It was at the Clothes Show in December 2007 that we realised our brand was namechecked on the GCSE syllabus. Moreover, within the last few months it's been drawn to our attention that we are a case study on the A-Level syllabus; and we already knew of the scrutiny we were attracting in the final theses of degree students. It has enabled us to have a high level of interns, as through their studies, students are made aware of our brand and ethics, as sustainability in style is a very important factor for upcoming designer-makers.

junky workshops

We have always loved the idea of sharing the Junky Ethos and spreading the recycled love, so we were happy to realise that there was a market for us and our methods!

We firstly took part in a workshop as part of a BBC initiative, and it was from there that we realised the levels of satisfaction that could be achieved all round, for both us and the participators. This progressed to myself and Anni talking at different educational events.

We were then offered the amazing opportunity for the whole team to take part in an event called Hackers and Heretics in Istanbul, which was curated by Otto von Busch and held at Pelin's lovely Garanti Gallery. The four of us went over and had the most amazing time, and it was then that we learnt that these types of events were one of our strengths. This was September 2008.

Since then we have begun going into different schools and doing workshops. It is great that the green agenda is such a prominent part of each school curriculum. Our job is to educate the kids in the hands-on element, so that they'll be able to put their knowledge into practice, to learn from us how to see reclaimed pieces differently and to look for the beauty in things that have already been produced.

It is still a learning process for us, and doesn't take up as much of our time as we'd like, but this will change as soon as we have locked down the perfect structure and the format will be rolled out on a wider scale.

Our current high profile workshop that we are involved with is Vinspired. com – A national incentive to inspire 16-24 year olds to volunteer their time to help others (all pieces created in the workshops are auctioned for charity), while learning recycling skills and gaining inspiration for future projects.

ethos, store
&buying trends

junky store
& buying trends

junky store
& buying trends

OPPOSITE Brace and suspenders created from a Tuxedo jacket. Photo by Martin Edwards.

TRADE SHOWS

As a multi-brand store that represents amazing individual labels, we were always invited as buyers to various trade shows, the first being a very pioneering show called 40 Degrees, where we learnt the nature of buying. Over time we have realised how different our style of buying has become.

Traditionally, a buyer will spend their entire budget twice a year, according to the seasons, on forward ordering. This means buying in February next season's Autumn/Winter stock for delivery in August, and again in September for the following season's Spring/Summer stock, with delivery in February, and so on. We initially attempted to get involved in the wholesale world by taking part in various trade shows ourselves in both London (TBC and Margin) and Paris (Workshop) – but to no real avail. We managed to pick up a few accounts, but the environment was never really conducive to the development of our brand. Because the nature of our clothes meant that no two pieces/materials were the same, our rails of clothes looked disjointed and 'un-collection-like', so we didn't fit in with the other brands, whose ranges flowed along the rails. We also offered not minimum but maximum order numbers, as everything we do is handmade, with the obvious limitations on capacity. A combination of being new to the wholesale market and just being in the wrong arenas for buyers to be able to understand the nature of our business meant that at that point in our evolution we were unable to succeed in getting our brand out there.

Then a major change occurred. A new movement came about at the stands of London Fashion Week at the Natural History Museum with the birth of Esthetica, the brainchild of Orsola and Filippo of From Somewhere. They created a space within the museum where ethical businesses that worked in an unconventional way could showcase their styles in a trade-show environment – an amazing development for all design-led recycled, fair-trade and organic companies.

The first show of this kind happened the season earlier at So Ethic at Prêt à Porter, Paris in February '06. We showed there, too, the show being an environment of education about our sector's ways of manufacture, as it would be later in London. This massive change enabled us to grow, winning new accounts and operating in both a short-order and rolling-order capacity, in line with both our manufacturing capabilities and the nature of our new customers. An impatient world had fallen upon us. Customers didn't want to have to wait five months to see new collections in-store; they wanted a higher turnover of variety and style – now.

In our shop we were able to give them want they wanted. We were able to produce a constant turnover of new, fresh styles in-house, daily, which was more than could be said for most other labels. We could begin creating a piece in the morning, and could then have sold it by the end of trading. It sometimes got to the point that if it was a freezing day in summer, we would make jumpers then and there, enabling us to battle with the ever-changing climate and seasons. And this was a USP for us when trying to create new accounts in the wholesale market. Our production methods allowed us to strike positive business relations directly with the buyer, as we had flexibility. Not only could we assure them that each piece they received from us would never be seen in any other store (in itself an amazing point-of-sale story), but we were able to respond to the needs of those same buyers individually throughout the season, recreating the same designs in fabrics of their choice, directly reacting to the marketplace and individual orders.

All this meant that our unique way of producing clothes, coupled with our non-seasonal yet timeless designs, allowed us to stand a chance as a small brand in an ever-changing consumer climate.

The London Fashion Week trade show.

wholesale

JUNKY HAS BEEN SOLD IN:

Amsterdam

Athens

Barcelona

Beirut

Belfast

Bologna

Copenhagen

Dublin

The Hague

Mantova

Milan

Paris

Riyadh

Rome

Sarasota

Stockholm

Tokyo

Vienna

Zurich

UK

Brighton

Coventry

Kendal

Liverpool

Chiswick, London

Islington, London

New Cross, London

Oxford Street, London

Westbourne Grove, London

Middlesbrough

Nottingham

Stockport

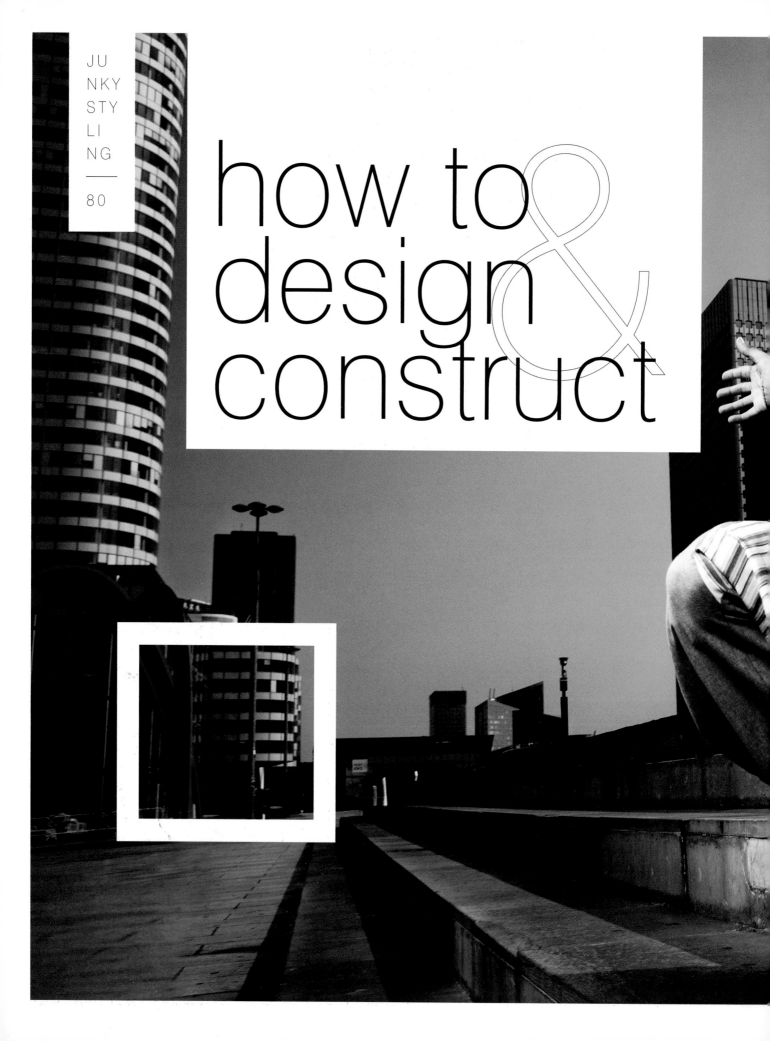

how to design & construct

Recycling, reusing, reconstruction, transformation, customisation – call it what you want. We've always considered what we do at Junky to be 'recycling clothing for the future'.

Recycling worn, discarded, second-hand clothing involves taking a garment that already has an identity and looking at it as a raw material, studying the existing form and details, then applying them to a new design – a complete reinterpretation and disregard for the existing identity of the piece. This involves a vision and an understanding of form and functionality.

We reckon that you can recycle anything, and it's a wonderful way to engage our imaginations. With such a vast array of materials used in clothing, we have always maintained the distinction between 'natural' and 'manmade' fabric. The quality of natural textiles has always made them first choice for our raw materials. Our first clothing creation was made from a pure-wool grey pinstripe suit; the feel, strength and durability of the cloth impressed and continues to inspire us. The cloth also helped to define the identity of Junky Styling as a 'new take on tailoring'. With no attention paid towards promoting an image or branding, the raw materials spoke for themselves and showed that Junky Styling was all about lasting quality and sustainability.

'Recycling is extending the life of an item. Nothing exceeds its 'sell-by date' – the date just changes and keeps changing, continually updating until the fabric falls apart.

Despite being a pioneer in London for recycling in the fashion industry, we at Junky Styling are under no illusion that we 'started' anything. Clothing recycling has been going on for a very long time.

clothes rationing during WWII

Clothes were rationed during the Second World War, just like food, petrol and soap. Beginning on 1 June 1941, everyone was allowed 66 clothing coupons a year, which more or less added up to one complete outfit a year.

Clothes bought from the shops were designed to use as little material as possible. On a men's suit you would have only three pockets, no turn-

PREVIOUS PAGE
Le Parkour. Photo by Marian Sell.

OPPOSITE
Mannequin. Photo by Ness Sherry.

ups, only three buttons and a maximum trouser length of 48 cm (19 in.). On the dress for women, there would be no elastic waistbands, no fancy belts and a maximum heel height of 5 cm (2 in.). For a nightdress you would have to pay with 6 coupons; for a men's overcoat, 16 coupons; for a dress, 11 coupons; as well as 8 coupons for pyjamas, 4 coupons for underpants and half a coupon for a handkerchief.

Women were encouraged to repair and remake their family's old clothes. Old curtains were cut up to make skirts and dresses. Unwanted jumpers were unravelled and knitted into something else.

junky suits

We have always favoured old men's suits as the basis of our raw materials for recycling. This formal uniform of the City of London has always inspired the most innovative of our designs. The fact that our shop and studio are so close to the heart of the City is an added bonus and makes for a great juxtaposition. The creations we produce belie the original identity of a suit, and

RIGHT Cotton reels from studio. Photo by Ness Sherry.

ABOVE A Junky trademark – structured suit jacket. Photo by Ness Sherry.

challenge the traditional image of how to wear one.

For the last ten years we have explored every element of the suit jacket, trouser and shirt, and we still feel there is potential for so many more designs.

We don't completely limit our raw materials, however, and we happily use T-shirts, knitwear, gabardine macs, dress fabrics such as rayon, linen and chiffon, silk smoking jackets, coats made from techno-fabrics, vintage ties, denim – anything in fact – but our design inspiration always comes from what we create out of suits and shirts.

The main skills required are imagination, patience and sheer determination. Always finish what you start or you'll end up with lots of failed experiments and unfinished projects.

On the following pages we have listed some of our most popular recycled creations – separated into jackets, trousers and shirts – and we've also picked out some designs for you to try yourself.

DES
IGN
&CO
NST
UCT

———

finding raw materials

re·design

shopping list
for budding
clothing recyclers

A RANGE OF RAW MATERIALS IS NEEDED. WE SUGGEST FINDING THE FOLLOWING ITEMS TO GET STARTED:

Cotton shirt
Jacket
Vintage dresses
Stretchy tops
Trousers
Long wide skirts
Tight-knit wool jumpers
Cardigans
Silk scarves
Coats
Bed sheets
Table cloths

THE RECYCLER'S STUDIO, BE IT YOUR BEDROOM OR ANY OTHER SPACE, SHOULD HAVE THE FOLLOWING ESSENTIAL TOOLS:

Scissors
Scapel or stitch-unpicker
Threads
Pins and needles
Sewing machine
Bias binding and ribbon/tape
Steam iron
Tape measure and ruler
Mannequin or tailor's dummy
Buttons
Velcro
Elastic
Tailor's chalk or pencil
Notepad
Mirror

PREVIOUS PAGE Le Parkour, shot in Paris. Photo by Marian Sell.

OPPOSITE Original art by Cept148, from our Kensington Market stall, recycled into 'Cotton Man' for the studio.

shopping for second-hand clothes & finding raw materials

When you decide to make something for yourself you will probably be inspired by something you already have or want for your wardrobe. Depending on what garment that is, you will need to follow certain rules when looking for raw materials.

SHIRTS Check armpits, collars, cuffs and buttonholes for wear and stains. If it's stretchy or sheer material it may be hard to cut and sew. Cotton is a safe bet because it's a natural, breathable, stable fabric.

TROUSERS Crutch and upper thighs are the problem areas. Always turn the garment inside out to check properly, and hold them up to the light to see worn areas. Remember to check that the zip works well.

JACKETS Check the collar, cuffs, hem and lining for worn and stained areas. Bobbles can sometimes be found on the inner arms and sides of a jacket. Frayed buttonholes can mess up a design.

KNITWEAR Look for moth-holes and bobbles. Jumpers can get baggy and stitches can loosen over time.

SKIRTS AND DRESSES Weak seams can ruin an expanse of fabric. The darts on the backs of skirts can get stretched and needle damage appears. Check armholes on dresses for the condition of the cloth. Hemlines sometimes suffer wear and tear.

COATS The first thing to 'go' is the lining, specifically in the armholes and hems. Coats have a lot of fabric and details to work with. Macs are brilliant sources of button fastenings, belts and pocket details. They are also made from durable fabric, but unfortunately they are also often beige!

VINTAGE FABRICS If you are lucky you may find lengths of vintage fabric. Open these out fully and check for holes, stains, sun damage and frayed areas. This applies to scarves, shawls, tablecloths and bed linen.

OPPOSITE Helenie and model in the basques and shirt wrap skirts. Photo by Luz Martin.

deconstructing garments

OPPOSITE Helenie models pieces from our S/S 08 collection. Photo by Ness Sherry.

✳ Use a scalpel, carefully!

✳ Hold the seam open, by pulling it apart with your fingers, and get the scalpel into the line of the stitching, then slide the blade along in short strokes to cut through the row of stitches.

✳ When choosing seams to unpick, avoid the seam that runs into the cuff of a sleeve, in case you destroy this feature. Also, steer clear of seams that run into box pleats on the backs of jackets, if you want to keep the pleats. Don't unpick the seams that run through the front of a jacket into the pocket, as you will then be unable to use the pocket.

✳ When you unpick the top layer of suiting, remember to unpick the corresponding seams in the lining.

✳ When removing a waistband, always check to see if the ends are separate to the fly on the inside, or you won't be able to fully detach it.

✳ When you remove collars and cuffs that are two layers of fabric, slice the stitches on the side that has visible top-stitching – this way, both sides of the fabric will disconnect at the same time.

✳ You may want to cut rather than unpick when it comes to shirts, as you can waste valuable time unpicking French seams.

✳ Unpicking knitwear is very difficult and often results in unravelling the wool either side of the sections you are trying to deconstruct. The best thing to do is cut the seams off completely and you are left with the different sections intact.

✳ Have a steam iron handy to press the garment you are about to deconstruct. Keep pressing each section as you take it apart.

RAW
MAT
ERI
ALS

___

sewing tips

✻ Make sure your machine is threaded correctly. You will find a diagram in the manual, or if you don't have the manual, take the machine into a local sewing-machine shop and ask.

✻ Try to match the cotton to the garment colour as closely as you can.

✻ Always use the same thread in your bobbin as the thread you are stitching with. Otherwise, you may have tension issues and snags in your stitching.

✻ When using pins, place them at a right angle to the line of stitching you intend to sew. You can sew straight over the tops of pins if you are sewing vertically across a horizontal line of pins, but never sew over them if they are placed in the same direction as your sewing line.

✻ Sew back and forth over the same spot when you start and finish a row of stitching, so as to keep the row of stitching from unravelling.

✻ You should change the size of the needle according to what you are sewing. If you are sewing a light silk, chiffon or even cotton, a small, slim needle is required, but if you are sewing denim, use a fatter, heavier needle.

✻ Use a zipper foot when putting in a zip.

✻ When you are lining a garment, 'bagging out' is a great tip for neat finishing. Sew two fabrics together with the wrong sides visible and then turn the fabric through to the right sides, leaving the raw seam trapped inside between the two layers.

✻ Always leave a centimetre for your seam allowance, and keep this in mind when you are cutting your sections out or the finished garment may end up too small.

✻ Take your time and enjoy yourself. Happy sewing!

OPPOSITE Anni at work. Photo by Luz Martin.

junky
essentials

the suit jacket

OPPOSITE Junky loves to recycle suit jackets. The lapel dress from 'Show Off' is a fine example of this.

You gain a great understanding of patterns and garment construction through unpicking and dissecting an item of tailored clothing, in this case, the suit jacket. Examples of all the new designs that can be made are listed below.

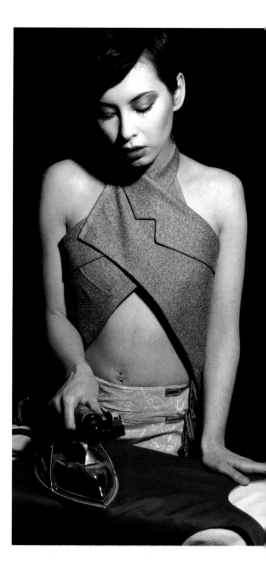

CROSSOVER TOP

The two front panels of a men's jacket are removed from the body of the jacket though still attached to the collar. They are then crossed over the front of the body and buttoned to the back with the original button fastenings, resulting in a tailored halter neck that splits at the front.

FREESTYLE LAPEL

The lapel is cut away and trimmed so that it wraps behind the neck and under the arms, fastening at the back with either a button section or a big bow made from shirting.

BASQUES

We have made many variations on fully boned basques. The basis of all of them is a five-panelled design that plays on the existing features of the jacket used as the raw material; for example, the breast pocket or collar will form part of the shape of the basque. They all tend to lace at the back in a crisscross effect, and all have six supporting bones on each seam.

SOFT-BACK BASQUES

The expanse of fabric on the back of the jacket is taken and mixed with a soft cotton stretch rib, to make a boob tube with a tailored-front effect.

CROPPED SLEEVES

This is a mini-jacket design, a pattern that we lay flat onto a deconstructed suit jacket and cut out, retaining all the best tailoring features. They look fantastic with our basques.

HOT PANTS

This is a pattern applied to a deconstructed jacket which retains the features of the original garment. The tailored fabric of a suit jacket lends

ABOVE The crossover top was the first Junky design ever made way back in 1998. Photo by Luz Martin.

PREVIOUS PAGE Portrait shot by Luz Martin. Michael Costiff and beautiful girls on the catwalk. Photo by Duncan Bone.

JU
NKY
ESS
ENT
IALS

itself well to this simple design, and is a substantial-enough fabric for such a skimpy item. These pants are best worn by girls with 'killer' legs, as these are exposed from the tops of the thighs down.

HALTER WAISTCOAT

This is a very simple design comprising the existing collar and front panels of a suit jacket, cut and shaped for a woman's body and tied with a bow at the back. The sexiness of this design when it's worn by a woman is such that it subverts the original garment that it is constructed from. We also do a masculine men's version that does up with a waistcoat buckle.

SUIT-BOTTOM SKIRT

Half a suit jacket is cut off and reshaped into an A-line skirt. A soft rib band with drawstring or elastic is added.

SUIT-JACKET HALTER DRESS

This is the full length of the jacket with the top half of the back and the sleeves cut away. It is fitted to the lower back and sides of the-bust and naturally splits at the front with the jacket fastening.

AUDREY DRESS

This design takes nearly a whole men's jacket and is a neat fitted dress with a side zip. The collar of the jacket is flipped round to the front to make a scooped neck, and the dress is slightly cut away at the back.

SUIT WRAP SKIRT

The suit jacket is deconstructed and panelled together to wrap around the hips and legs and fasten in a slanting button section to the front side of the skirt.

HOOD SCARF

The back section of the jacket is used to construct a hood, and the sleeves act as the wrapping section once they have been backed onto soft wool or lined in silk or cotton.

HOODED BOMBER JACKET

The collar and fastening of the jacket is removed and a zip placed all the way up the centre of the jacket. Sport-style cotton jersey is used to construct a hood and cuffs at the end of the sleeves. These are available for men and women.

CLOCKWISE FROM TOP LEFT
Men's Halter Waistcoat A man's halter waistcoat from 'community' show.
Halter Waistcoat and Jacket bottom One man's suit jacket is enough to construct the 'Jacket bottom shirt' and 'halter waistcoat'.
Basques A basque is a classic shape to work with and looks fabulous in bold fabrics such as vintage ties and silk scarves.
Freestyle lapel The freestyle lapel can give an edge to any outfit.
Suit Bomber The Suit Bomber is one of the best selling jackets from the Junky store. This one was featured in our 'Community' show.
Audrey Dress The Audrey dress quickly became a classic Junky dress.

HOODED WAISTCOAT

We use our waistcoat pattern on an old jacket to construct a traditional waistcoat. The back is made from an old shirt or lining fabric. We then give it a very contemporary twist by cutting a hood from the remnants of the jacket and attaching it to the neck of the waistcoat with a zip, so that it can be worn with or without the hood.

UD JACKET

This is simple but amazingly effective. We turn a jacket upside down and take the sleeves out, then reinsert them the opposite way up. The new neck section (previously the bottom of the jacket) is ruched to give structure and make a wide-textured draping collar. The lapel of the jacket is now positioned across the ribcage and fastens below the bust.

FULL JACKET DRESS

This stunning design comes from all the design features of a jacket deconstructed and crafted into a sexy layered dress. The opened sleeves are placed on the hips and the body is constructed out of the back panels of the jacket. It laces like a bodice across the back.

SUIT-SLEEVE SCARF

The sleeves of a suit jacket are cut off to make the ends of an easy-to-wear scarf. These are fused together using fabric from the back of the jacket lined in a complementary softer fabric, which rests against the back of the neck.

See Design Formulas: UD jacket, suit sleeve scarf.

suit sleeve
scarf

The following instructions will guide you through the process of making your own sleeve scarf. This design can be worn by men and women, is easy to slip into any wardrobe and will add a stylish collar to any jacket or coat.

LEFT
Michael, photo taken by Stefan Svens.

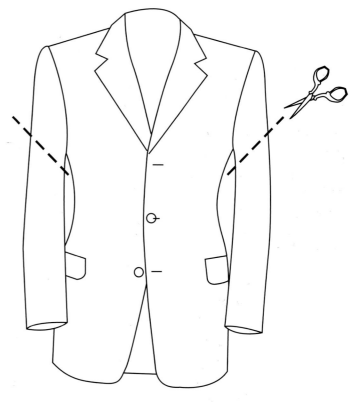

1 Take a suit jacket and some wool or sweatshirt material. Cut the sleeves off the jacket straight across under the arm to get maximum length; they should be about 43 cm (17 in.) long. Press them flat and 'stay stitch' lining to sleeve fabric.

2 Cut the fabric for the middle of the scarf section in two pieces at the same width as the sleeve and approximately 50 cm (20 in.) in length. You can vary this length.

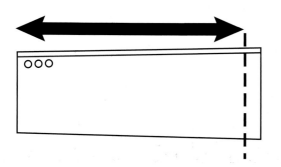

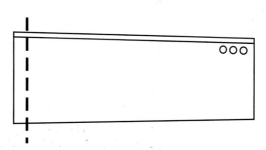

3 Sew the scarf pieces together along the long sides and turn them through so you end up with a tube of fabric.

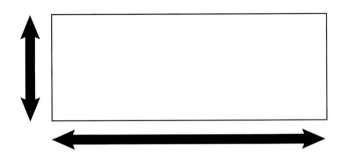

4 Sew the sleeves into each of the open ends of the tube of fabric. One sleeve should have buttons facing you and the other should have buttons facing the other side, away from you.

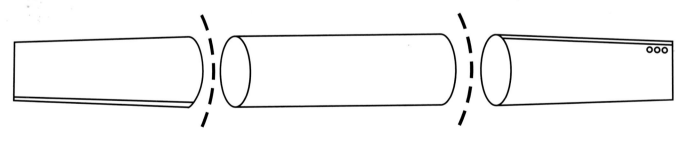

5 Flip over the side with the buttons facing away by 18 cm (7 in.), so that the buttons on each sleeve are facing you.

6 Sew in place through all the layers of the sleeve. Slot the straight sleeve through the folded-back sleeve.

T his design reinvents the shape of a jacket by turning it upside down. The result is a jacket with a luxurious draping collar and fitted waist, whilst retaining a tailored feel to the garment. Try using the jacket from an old suit to update the whole outfit.

1 Take a small suit jacket (ladies' preferably). Unpick the sleeves and the lining from the armholes.

2 Take in the shoulder seams on each side like darts, 5 cm (2 in.) deep at the shoulder reducing to nothing under the collar. Trim away the excess and press open the new shoulder seam. Do the same to the corresponding lining seam.

3 Iron the collar flat and turn it upside down. Lay flat and use the narrowed armhole to recut the sleeve heads on the arms.

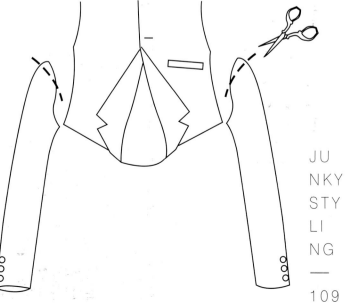

4 Sew the outer layer of the sleeves to the outer layer of the armholes, raw edges on the inside of the garment. Split open the lining to get inside, and sew the sleeve linings to the armhole linings.

5 Ruche or pleat the centre back seam from what was previously the bottom of the jacket to about halfway down (this will be at the back of the neck when worn).

Repeat this rouching/pleating up the side seams to the top of shoulder.

6 Either try on the jacket or place it on a mannequin and mark the new button placement. You may want to attach loops or ties to create new fastenings on either side of the original buttonholes.

Finally, add new sparkly buttons.

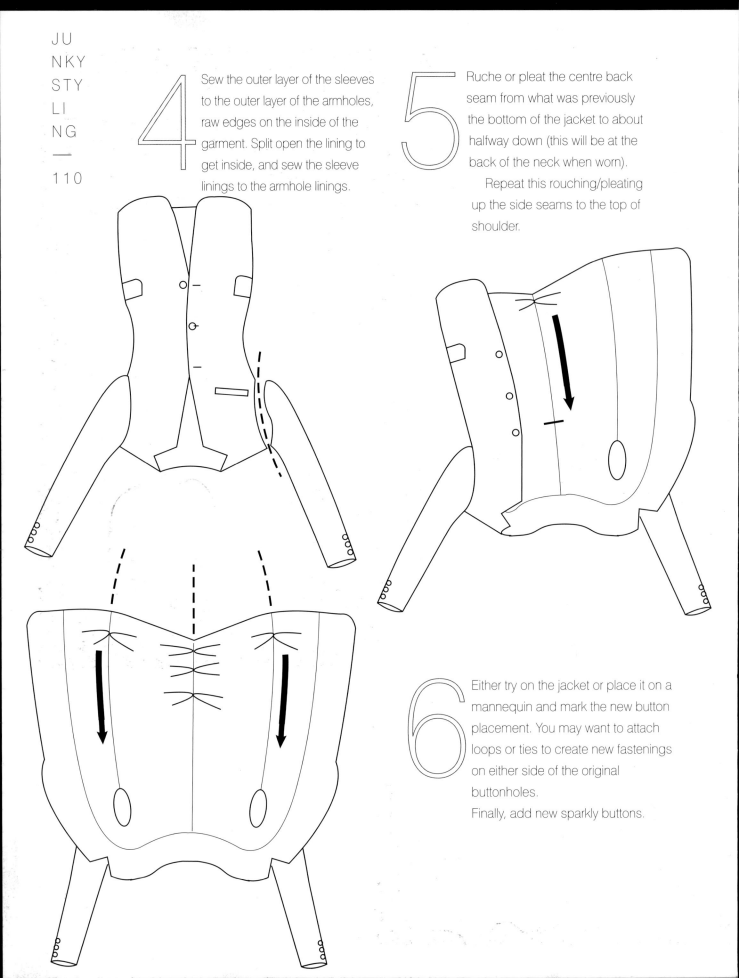

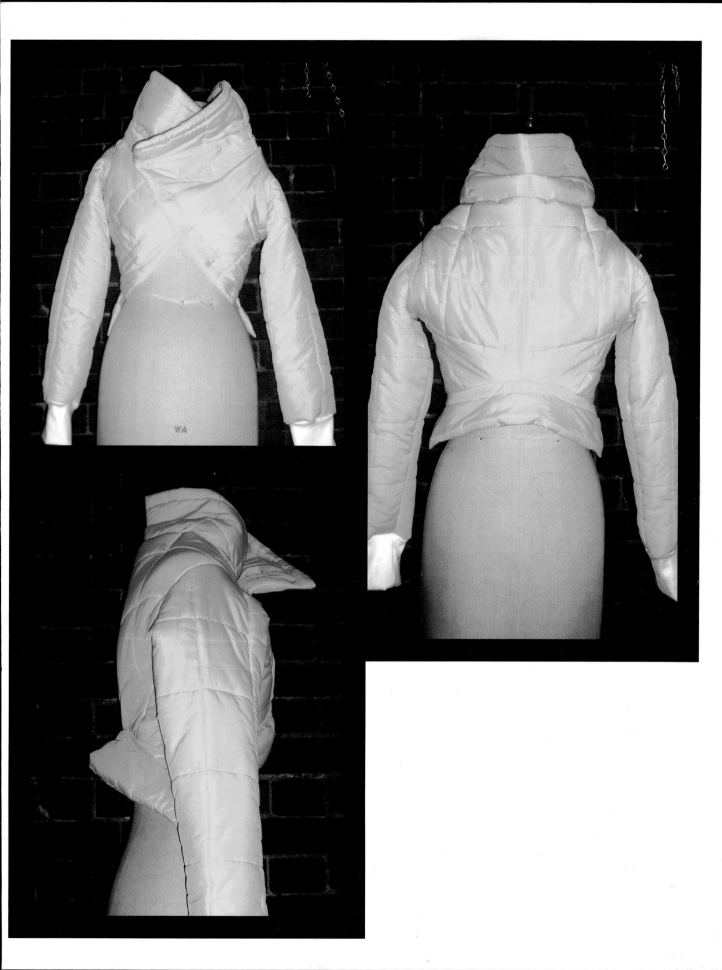

trousers

The features on the average pair of trousers that lend themselves to a new garment are the waistband, the fly and the good large expanses of fabric that make up the legs.

FLY TOP

The waistband wraps around the back and shoulders so that the fly sits on the centre of the collar running down the chest. Armholes are created where the pockets would previously have been. The top section is drawn into a stretchy tube that starts just under the bust and runs down to the waist or hips.

ABOVE Everybody wears trousers, especially when they've been transformed by Junky.

OPPOSITE **High Waisted Trouser** Our classic high waisted trouser shown at our 'community' show. **Ladies Hareems** The Hareem trousers make a fluid design for ladies.

TROUSER DRESS

This dress has a halter neck consisting of the waistband (complete with belt loops) coming around the back of the neck and down into a low V-neck at the centre front. The full length of the trousers is pleated into each side of the chest and the rest of the fabric wraps around the hips to the middle of the lower back, where a zip is then inserted; ties are often attached to give extra fit and security.

HAREEMS

Two pairs of trousers are completely unpicked along the outer legs and back of waistband. One pair has the fly, pockets and waistband section removed, and is then fused to the other pair, creating double-width legs and a long hanging crutch section that buttons up to several different heights on the bum.

CUFF PUSHERS

Cuffs are cut from a suit jacket at about 15–20 cm (6–8 in.) long, opened up and sewn flat, then attached to each hem of a pair of trousers that have been shortened to peddle-pusher length.

HIGH-WAISTED TROUSERS/SHORTS

Two pairs of suit trousers are cut to our pattern and fused together to make a long-leg trouser with an extended-length button-through waistband. The back jet pockets are cut and repositioned on the thigh panel. The waistband section can be unbuttoned and flipped down to create a hipster trouser.

SWOOSH SKIRT/ BACK 2 BACK DRESS

Lengths of fabric taken from trouser legs are all sewn together to make two big squares of fabric. These can then be trimmed into circles to make a 'swoosh', or remain as squares to make a 'back 2 back' skirt. The two pieces of fabric are then sewn together around the edges and a hole is cut through the double layer. These holes are connected on the inside of the garment with a stretchy jersey tube that forms part of the waistband. This becomes a full-bodied skirt with a visible under-section.

ABOVE
High Waisted Shorts
The shorter version gives a stylish proportion to the high waist.

Magic Trousers The 'magic trouser' was the corner stone of the first ever Junky collection.

OPPOSITE
Cuff Pushers with UD Jacket.

MAGIC TROUSERS

This was the first ever Junky design. The waistband is unpicked on a pair of suit trousers and then the bottom half of a suit jacket is sewn under to the top edge of the trouser. The waistband is reattached, trapping the jacket to make a short wraparound skirt section hanging from the waist. Loved by both men and women, magic trousers are a great way to wear a suit without being traditional.

JU
NKY
ESS
ENT
IALS

—

CIRCLE SKIRT

Several trouser legs are cut off at the thighs. They are then sewn together along the sides of the trousers so that the narrow part (hem) is at one end and the wider part is at the other. This shape curves to form a skirt, with the wide edge becoming the bottom of the skirt and the hem edge being drawn/pleated into an elasticated belt or the previous waistband adjusted to size.

See Design Formulas: circle skirt, fly top.

ABOVE Swoosh skirt.

OPPOSITE The Back 2 Back Dress is a stunning transformation of trousers. Photo by Ness Sherry.

step by step

the fly top

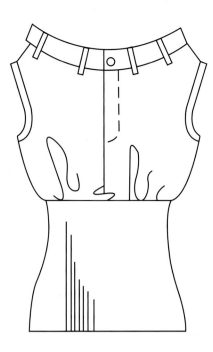

With these step by step instructions you can turn any pair of trousers into a fitted top with a wide structured neck line with a zip detail. The fitted waist accentuates the shape of the top section and flatters the figure.

1 Take a pair of trousers and a stretchy T-shirt or vest. Hold the waistband of the trousers against your shoulders to check for size. Fold the trousers in half so that the back pockets are flat against each other and the fly is on the edge of the fold.

2 Cut across from the crotch point (just below the fly) straight out to the side. Cut through all layers and make sure the pockets are clear of the cut lines.

You may want to straighten out the curve of the crotch seam under the fly by sewing straight down.

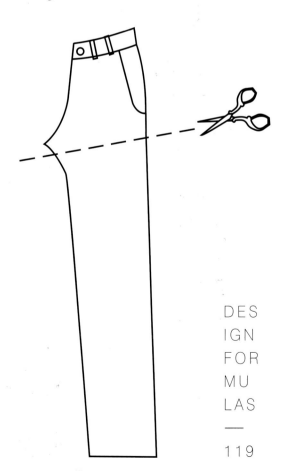

3 Still folded in half, cut armholes at the side where the pockets are. Cut through any pockets.

4 Cut your vest or T-shirt straight across the back and chest under the armholes. Cut through front and back simultaneously.

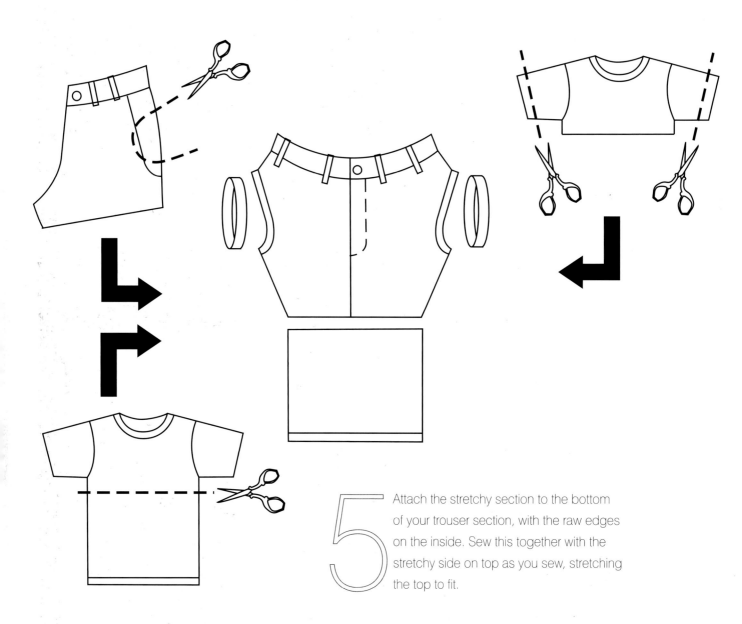

5 Attach the stretchy section to the bottom of your trouser section, with the raw edges on the inside. Sew this together with the stretchy side on top as you sew, stretching the top to fit.

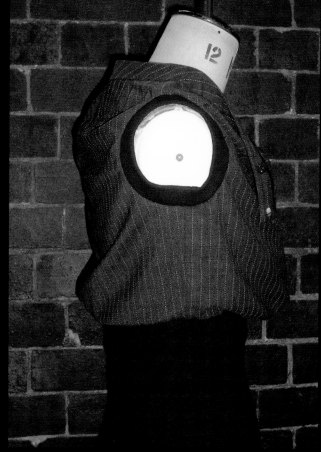

For the trim on the armholes, cut two strips of the remaining off-cuts of the T-shirt or vest (you can take part of the sleeve if you have used a T-shirt). Make these strips a bit longer than half the length of the armhole (when laid out flat) and 5 cm (2 in.) wide. Sew together the 5 cm (2 in.) widths on each strip, creating two circles. Fold these halfway in all the way round, creating two complete circles with a folded edge (this is a raw edge). Attach these to the armholes, raw edges to the inside of the garment and folded edge to the outside. Keep the pockets flat and in place as you stretch on the armhole trim.

step by step

circle skirt

This skirt is not quite a circle of trouser legs but is based on the 50's classic 'circle skirt'. The basic instructions can be taken further and more trouser legs can be used to add fullness.

1 Take at least three pairs of trousers (this will make a 12-section skirt). Fold in half with legs flat and back pockets facing each other. Cut the thigh section straight across at the widest part.

2 Next cut from the outer corners of the bottom of the trouser legs in a diagonal long cut all the way to the outer edges of the thigh. Remove all outer seams of the trousers which will leave you with wedges of trouser-leg fabric with one narrow end and one wide end.

Cut the lengths of these sections all the same.

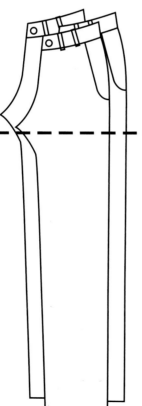

3 Sew the long sides together with all the short ends at the same side, creating a curve in the expanse of fabric you are sewing together.

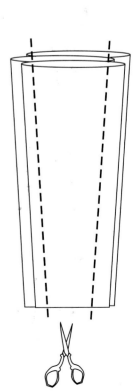

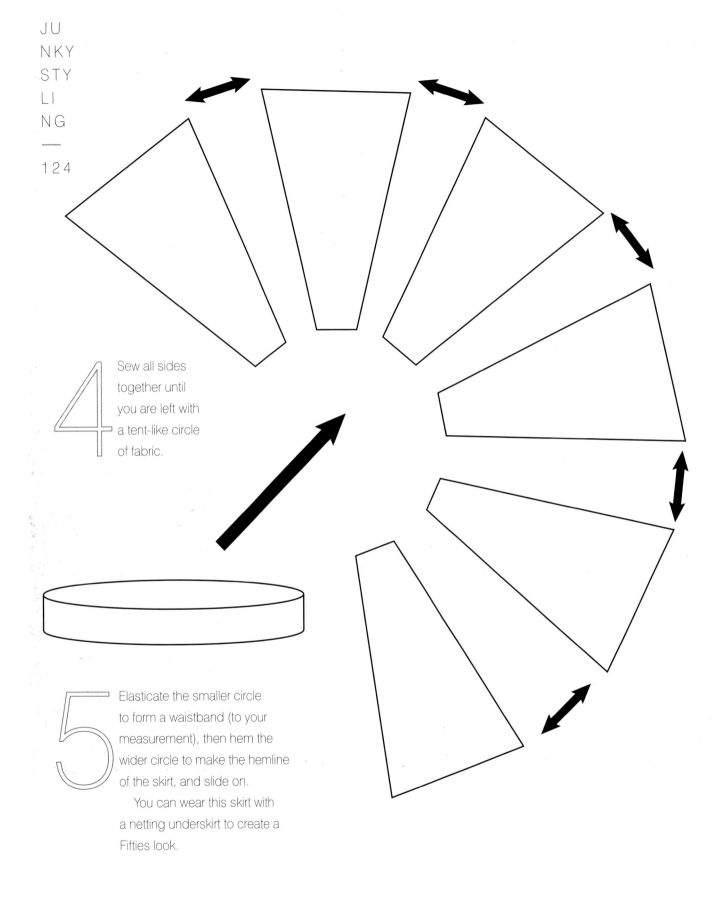

4 Sew all sides together until you are left with a tent-like circle of fabric.

5 Elasticate the smaller circle to form a waistband (to your measurement), then hem the wider circle to make the hemline of the skirt, and slide on.

You can wear this skirt with a netting underskirt to create a Fifties look.

shirts

ABOVE Shirts.

OPPOSITE Swoosh Dress
from shirts for the S/S 07
collection.
Photo by Ness Sherry.

Formal men's cotton shirts tend to be the mainstay of Junky's summer fabric and raw materials to create garments from. The potential of this item is limitless, and the colours, patterns, cuts and weights of cotton all inspire new designs, as do the details such as collars, cuffs, button plackets (button strip), epiletts and pockets. Listed below are just a few examples of what we do with shirts.

HAREEM SHORTS

The shirt placket runs down the centre of a low-slung crotch. The sleeves are splayed open to form the sides of the legs, ending in cuffs which sit at the knees. The remainder of the shirt is used to make the baggy seat of the shorts at the back. The waist is elasticated; the shorts are designed to be worn at the hip in a slouchy fashion.

TWIN-SPIN/TRIPLE-SPIN SKIRT

Two (twin) or three (triple) halves of the fronts of different shirts are attached to a soft stretchy rib waistband. These are either all the button sides or all the buttonhole sides, which in turn creates a 'spin' effect.

SHIRT-SLEEVE BUSTIER

The front is styled from the back of the shirt while the back is a soft stretch-rib jersey. The sleeves are layered across the top of the front, with the cuffs central. The bustier is a strapless tube shape.

SHIRT SWOOSH SKIRT AND DRESS

The bottom halves of two shirts are cut off, opened up and sewn together to make a large expanse of fabric. These are cut into a circle and sewn all the way around the edge of another circle of fabric, which is the same size and a complementary colour or pattern. A central hole is cut through both layers and connected on the inside of the garment by a stretchy rib tube, which forms part of the waistband. A sash belt is made from the non-shirt fabric, and shirt cuffs are turned into big belt loops. We have also adapted this design into a dress by applying thick straps to make a halter neck.

SUMMER AUDREY DRESS

An entire shirt is used to construct this neat shift dress. The buttoning front section of a shirt is at the centre front of the dress, and the back of the shirt is cut and darted to form the back of the dress. The collar is reversed and frames a low scoop neck. The cuffs button across the back of the waist, and the dress has a side zip for access.

HIGH-WAISTED SHORTS/PENCIL SKIRT

Several shirts are cut into sections to make either shorts or a pencil skirt with a high-waist, with an overlapping four-button section (in the style of sailor trousers). Braces can be made from the remaining fabric to add a sassy edge to the look.

ONE-TIER SHIRT DRESS/TOP/SKIRT

This garment can be worn as a skirt or top. A shirt is turned upside down and the tail end blunted off. The cut end is frilled or pleated across the width, and the top section is sewn with shirring elastic to form a stretchy tube. If worn as a skirt, this stretch band clings to the hips, and the rest of the shirt hangs like a frilly skirt. Straps can be added if it's going to be a top, with the stretch on the bust and back and the rest flaring at the waist and hips. The sleeves can button up to the body in a looping fashion.

TWO OR THREE-TIER SHIRT DRESS

This is made with shirring elastic to fit to the upper body, with layers of shirts turned upside down and looping sleeves adding volume. Shirts of the same colour, or shirts in different, clashing colours, can be used for effect to construct this variable-length dress. We have made this design in white for a wedding dress, and it was used to represent Junky Styling in The Crafts Council exhibition Well Fashioned in 2006/7.

SHIRT CAPE

With the collar kept intact, the rest of the shirt is cut and sewn in a curve around the shoulders, covering the bust.

ELASTICATED SHIRT BOMBER JACKET

A whole shirt is recut into a bomber jacket. The collar of the jacket is made from the cuffs, and the waist and sleeve ends are elasticated.

CLOCKWISE FROM TOP LEFT
Shirt Hareems and sleeve scarf Shirt Hareems and shirt sleeve scarf from 'community' show – S/S 08 collection.
Swoosh skirt from shirts Swoosh Skirt from shirts for S/S 07 collection.
Summer Audrey dress Audrey dress from 'Cabriolet' S/S 06 collection.
Three Tier Shirt dress Three Tier shirt dress from 'Junky Habits' show.
High waisted skirt from shirts High Waisted looks from 'Community' show.
High waisted shorts.

THE PARKA DRESS

A hood is cut from the front section of one shirt and attached to the neck of another shirt (with the collar removed). The body is drawn in at the waist by a thick stretchy belt, and a long zip is used to fasten the dress all the way up the front, where the button placket has been removed.

SHIRT BASQUE

A six-boned basque is constructed from sections of a shirt. We often feature a shirt pocket on the front section or retro ties along the seams. This piece laces up on the back with loops and a tie.

SIDEWAYS SHIRT TOP

A shirt is turned on its side, and the collar forms one armhole while the open, draping hem forms the other. The entire arm and armpit are cut away to make a slash neck, and the whole body is drawn into a tight waist with stretchy rib.

HOODED SHIRT SCARF

Sleeves complete with cuffs make up the scarf section with the hood cut from the front section of the shirt. The buttons and buttonholes frame the edge of the hood.

HOODED SHIRT

As with the parka dress, the hood is cut from the front of one shirt and attached to another that has had the collar removed. The buttons and buttonholes frame the hood and lead into the other button placket running down the front of the shirt. The cuffs from one shirt are sewn to the edge of the sleeves of the other one to create long sleeves, and a double pocket is often added.

STRAPLESS SHIRT DRESS

A stretchy drawstring section is the top part of the dress, with the button placket running down the centre and form defining the body of the garment. The rest of the shirt is arranged in a layered section around the hem. The shirtsleeves are anchored either side of the waist and tie at the back to accentuate it.

SHIRT WRAP SKIRT

A shirt is taken apart and re-crafted into a wraparound miniskirt with a crisscross lacing section on the side. This can be made from one shirt, or for a more interesting two-tone effect we use two. The shape of the skirt is fitted at the hips and pleated around the hem.

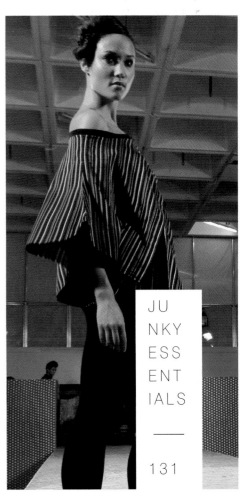

BUTTON-WAIST SKIRT WITH SLEEVE BOW

The placket of the shirt forms the waistband of the skirt. The back of the shirt is cut straight up the back, collar and shoulders removed, then it's turned on its side and this cut becomes the hem. The sleeves are cut and constructed into a bow, which sits on the side of the skirt that is ruched and sealed. The other side is sealed to fit, with two darts at the side of the waist. This design is hard to describe simply but relatively easy to make, and for this reason we have included it among the design formulas that you can try at home.

SHIRT WRAP HALTER TOP

The collar is reversed and buttons to the back of the neck, and the placket fastens to the lower back. The back of the shirt makes the front of the top, and the sleeves are pulled to the back from the sides of the waist to tie in a knot, which improves the fit. Again, we have included the design formula in this book so that you can transform any old shirt into this fantastic creation. Make it out of a black silk shirt for an evening look or use a bright stripy shirt to make a summer essential that's perfect with jeans.

See Design Formulas: sideways skirt with bow detail,
shirt wrap halter.

step by step

shirt wrap halter top

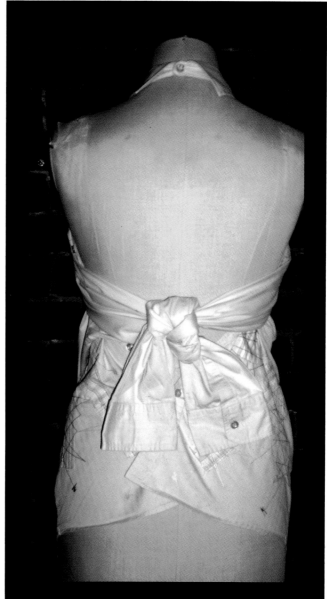

This creation is a great summer staple for any wardrobe. By cleverly and carefully reconstructing parts of a shirt so that it's worn backwards, you can make an adjustable halter top.

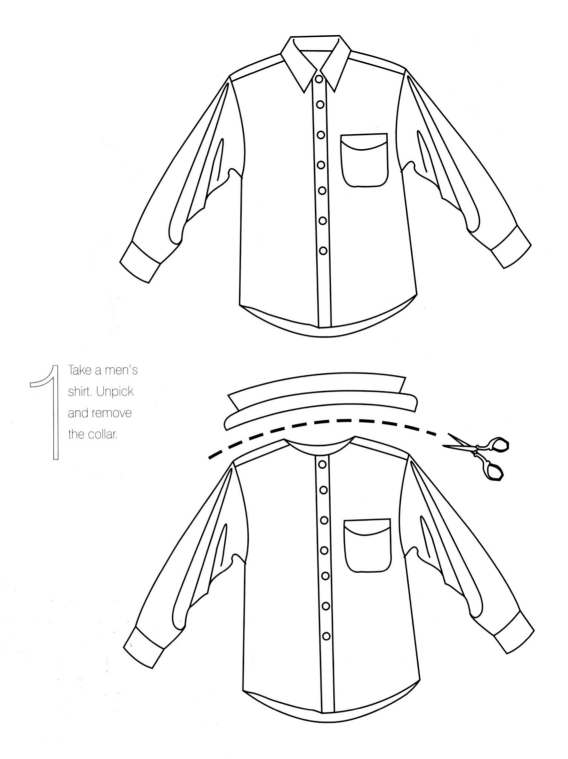

1 Take a men's shirt. Unpick and remove the collar.

2 Press the shirt, lay it front side down, and cut away at an angle from the hem at the side seam to 1 cm (0.4 in.) away from the side of the neck. Cut through the front and back simultaneously.

3 Cut the sleeves at an angle, with an underarm length of 48 cm (19 in.) and an overarm length of 64 cm (25 in.).

Stitch together the sleeves that you have just cut at angles in the front and back of the shirt, enclosing and attaching the sleeves 4 cm (1.5 in.) down from the yoke seam (the seam that runs across the back of the shoulders on a shirt).

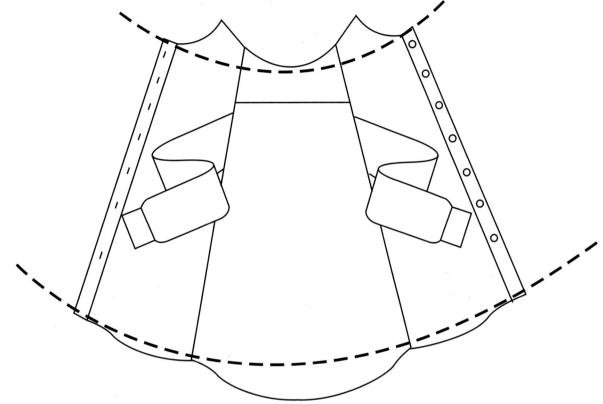

You can shorten the hemline according to the length of top you want. Reshape the neck by trimming away any unevenness, then gather it to approximately 20 cm (8 in.) in length.

Reattach the collar, placing the gathered section in the centre.

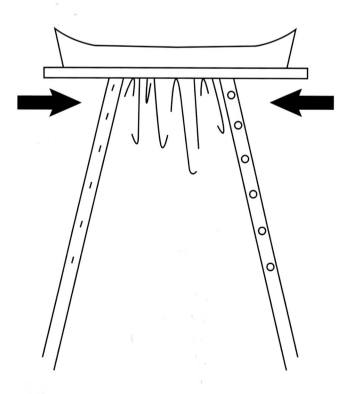

step
by
step

sideways skirt
with bow

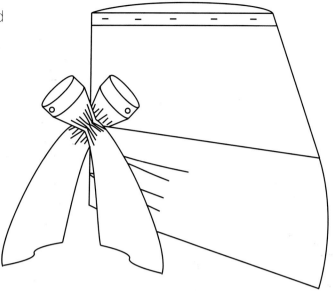

ever before have shirt sleeves created
such a dramatic swishing bow detail.
This enhances the simple skirt shape
constructed from the body of the shirt. The
button stand makes an adjustable waist for
this incredibly wearable piece.

1 Take a large men's shirt and lay it flat. Cut
around the armholes and in a straight line
across the shoulders above the top button on
the placket, thereby removing the entire collar.

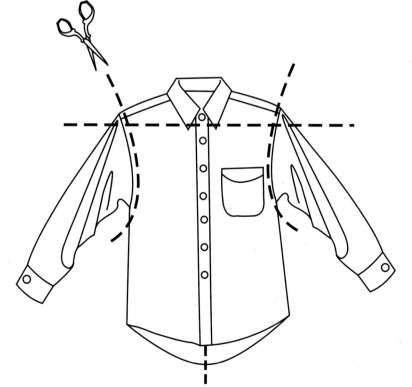

2 Open the back in one
straight central cut
from top to bottom.

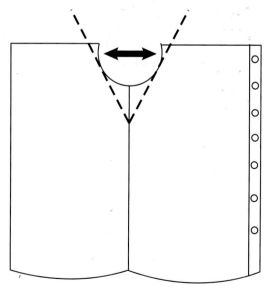

3 Close up the armhole on each side by folding it together, straightening off and sewing it into the side seams. This has a dart-like effect.

4 Turn the shirt on its side, with the buttonhole side of the placket at the front and the button side lying flat underneath. Overlock all the raw edges.

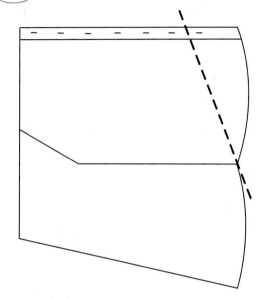

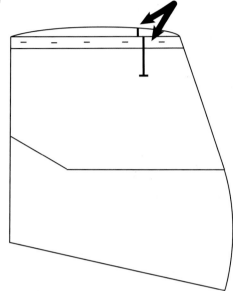

5 Sew together the side with the finished curve edge (formerly the bottom edge of the shirt) as far as the original side seam, halfway down in a diagonal line. This starts 1 cm (0.4 in.) away from the last button and buttonhole and gradually comes to meet the original side seam halfway down. Overlock any excess fabric from the inside.

6 Sew darts either side of the seam that has just been created. These are situated on each side, between the buttonholes and the buttons, and are 2 cm (0.8 in.) wide and 10 cm (4 in.) deep.

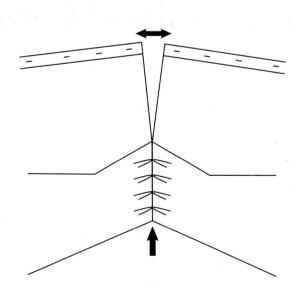

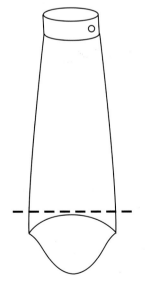

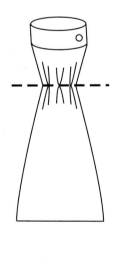

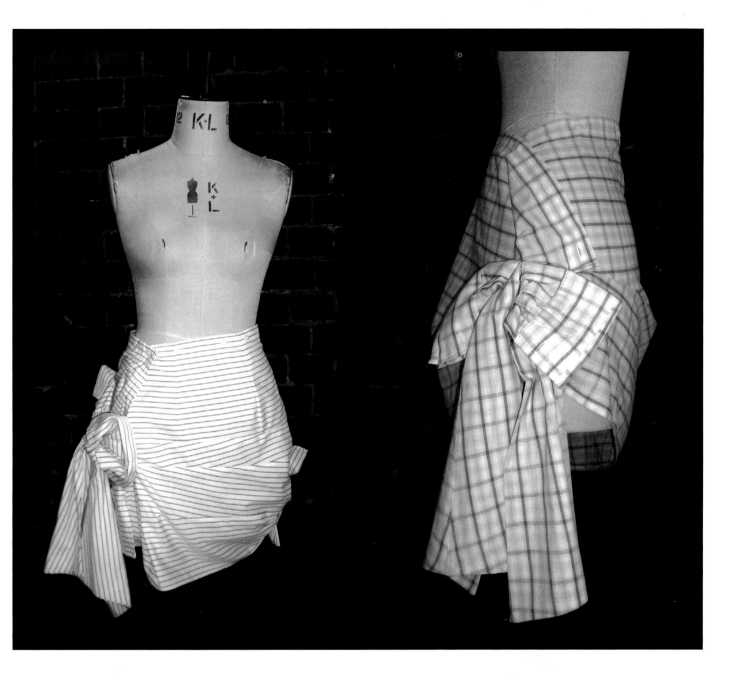

7 The other overlocked side will provide the access to get into the skirt, so leave a 15 cm (6 in.) opening. From this point down, join the sides together by pleating (ruching) the bigger edge to the smaller edge. This should finish at approximately 12 cm (4 in.) in length.

Stitch the edges of the opening flat to the inside.

8 Take the cut-off sleeves, turn them inside out and sew straight across (getting rid of the curved sleeve head). Turn back to the right side and ruche the sleeves 5 cm (2 in.) under the cuffs on each one. Lay one sleeve across the other at the ruched point and sew in place so that it resembles a bow shape.

Attach the bow-shaped sleeves to the ruched side at the bottom of the opening.

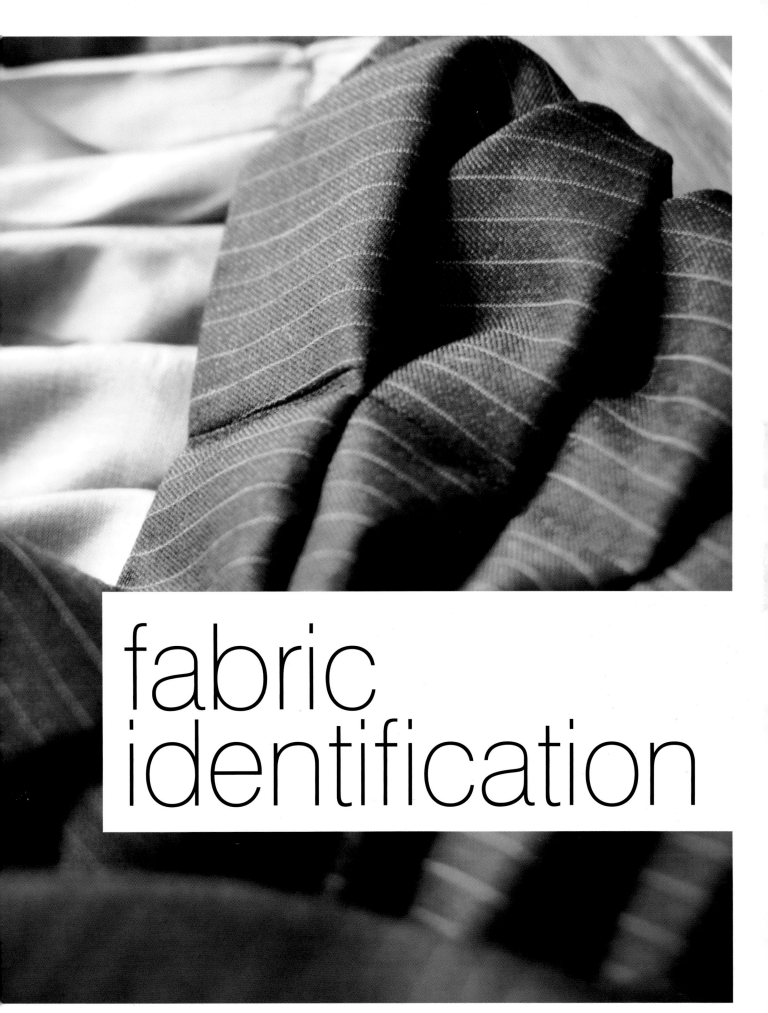

fabric identification

t's important to know what fabric you are working with so that you can decide how to store and care for your creation.

You can work out if the fabric you are using is a natural fibre, a manmade fibre or a mix of the two through a burn test.

For this, you must be careful and make sure you do the test in a non-plastic sink or metal bucket. Use a small piece of fabric, holding it with tweezers rather than fingers. Perform the test over a burnproof container like a metal dish containing an inch of water in the bottom. Certain fabrics could melt and drip, which could be very dangerous to your skin and damaging to surfaces.

ABOVE Cotton shirts.

**PREVIOUS PAGE
A pinstripe jacket
with rouching. Photo by
Ness Sherry.**

natural fabrics

COTTON is a plant fibre. When ignited it burns with a steady flame and smells like burning leaves. The ash left is easily crumbled. Small samples of burning cotton can be blown out as you would a candle.

LINEN is also a plant fibre but different from cotton in that the individual plant fibres which make up the yarn are long whereas cotton fibres are short. Linen takes longer to ignite. The fabric closest to the ash is very brittle. Linen is easily extinguished by blowing on it as you would a candle.

SILK is a protein fibre that usually burns readily, though not necessarily with a steady flame, and smells like burning hair. The ash is easily crumbled. Silk samples are not as easily extinguished as cotton or linen.

WOOL is also a protein fibre but is harder to ignite than silk, as the individual 'hair' fibres are shorter than silk and the weave of the fabrics is generally looser than with silk. The flame is steady but more difficult to keep alight. The smell of burning wool is like burning hair.

manmade fabrics

ACETATE is made from cellulose (wood fibres). Acetate burns readily with a flickering flame that cannot be easily extinguished. The burning cellulose drips and leaves a hard ash. The smell is similar to burning woodchips.

ACRYLIC is made from natural gas and petroleum. Acrylics burn readily due to the fibre content and the lofty, air-filled pockets. A match or cigarette dropped on an acrylic blanket can ignite the fabric, which will burn rapidly unless extinguished. The ash is hard and the smell is acrid or harsh.

NYLON is a polyamide made from petroleum. Nylon melts and then burns rapidly if the flame remains on the melted fibre. If you can keep the flame on the melting nylon, it smells like burning plastic.

POLYESTER is produced from coal, air, water, and petroleum products. Polyester melts and burns at the same time. Be aware that the melting, burning ash can bond quickly to any surface it drips on, including skin. The smoke from polyester is black with a sweetish smell. The extinguished ash is hard.

RAYON is a regenerated cellulose fibre. Rayon burns rapidly and leaves only a slight ash. The burning smell is close to that of burning leaves.

natural & manmade blended fabric

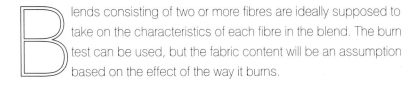

Blends consisting of two or more fibres are ideally supposed to take on the characteristics of each fibre in the blend. The burn test can be used, but the fabric content will be an assumption based on the effect of the way it burns.

cleaning & caring for your creation

When recycling you will probably have a manufacturer's label giving instructions on the proper care of the fabric. If there is no label, or if you wish to wash a garment or fabric at home instead of dry-cleaning it, the properties of each fabric will help you determine how to treat it.

DRY-CLEANING is by definition cleaning with solvents and little or no water. The combination of solvents and heat is hard on fabrics and may cause as much wear as the actual wearing of the garment. The solvents used are very effective but also toxic, so once you've had a garment dry-cleaned you should take it out of the plastic bag and air it. It is worth developing a dialogue with your dry-cleaner. Note the type of stains that you have on your garment and list them for the benefit of the dry-cleaner so that they can pre-spot them; this will help eliminate stains that could otherwise be heat-set into the fabric after the garment has been cleaned.

PRESSING after cleaning should also be considered. Most people can press wool trousers, but it takes a skilled professional presser to do a quality job on linen and silk items. Linen can withstand higher heat when ironed, and should be pressed when damp. Silk requires a lower-temperature iron and should be steam-ironed, preferably with a press cloth. Wool should be pressed with steam at a moderate temperature.

PACKAGING of the cleaned garment is also important. A garment can be cleaned and pressed well, but if it is then jammed into a small bag it could become a wrinkled mess.

PROFESSIONAL LAUNDERING is offered by most dry-cleaners. Washable garments are professionally washed and pressed. Men's and women's shirts are often bleached and starched according to the manufacturer's label. Some of the laundering is done with very hot water, which may shrink the interfacing or stiffening used in collars and cuffs. Less expensive garments may use interfacing that either shrinks or comes loose with very hot water. These garments cannot be fixed. Outer fabric, interfacings, linings, shoulder pads and finishes all react differently when washed. Some fabrics shrink or change shape when washed. Some shoulder pads are designed for dry-cleaning only, and may fall apart when washed.

STARCHING shirts and other cotton or cotton/polyester garments is common. The basic function of starch is to stiffen the garment. Its incidental use is in preventing stains from penetrating the fibre. However, starch leaves minute crystals in the fibre and can often wear out the garment more quickly than if it had not been starched. The choice for your garment, then, is appearance versus longer life.

HOME LAUNDERING is not only easier to control but can add life to your garments. Choose your detergent carefully and read the information on the package. Generally, the labels on the detergent inform you and make the choice easier. General-purpose laundry detergents work well on most washable fabrics. Added bleach may gradually remove the dyes or colour unless the garment is colourfast to bleach. More expensive is not always better.

SOAP is not the same as detergent. All detergents are soaps but not all soaps are detergents. Although soap has been improved over the years, it still leaves a deposit we call 'soap scum' in the shower and bath. This scum is difficult to remove from fabrics if soap is used in the laundry.

CHLORINE BLEACHES can be safely used on cotton, cotton/polyester and some manmade fabrics. Consult the garment-care label.

HAND-WASHING DETERGENTS can be used for home laundry when cleaning fine fabrics. These products are often effective when using cold water. However, not all hand-washing detergents are milder than regular laundry products, although they are often more expensive. Properties to look for when choosing a hand-washing detergent include its use in cold water, that it dissolves quickly in cold water, and that it can be completely rinsed after washing.

SHAMPOOS can also be used for hand-washing your garments. Use a good shampoo, not one containing 'creme rinse'. If your shampoo cleans your hair and leaves it shiny with no residues, it will usually clean your garment, too.

FABRIC SOFTENERS, both liquid and dryer sheets, add products/treatments to your fabrics. Some of the softeners are wax-based, which leaves a coating on the fibre, creating a softer feel but reducing the fibre's absorbency. Some softeners have a perfume that causes an allergic reaction in many people. If you have ever used a fabric-softener dryer sheet with your polyester garments, you may have seen 'grease' spots appear on your garment. This is actually a wax that can be removed by rewashing that garment.

the properties of manmade fabrics

Manufactured fabrics are usually made of filaments extruded as liquid and formed into various fibres. Because they start as a liquid, many of the fibres are coloured before they become filament, and thus they are difficult to dye after the fibre has been woven into a fabric.

ACETATE does not absorb moisture readily, but dries fast and resists shrinking. A resilient fabric, it resists wrinkling in addition to being pliable and soft with a good drape. Triacetate is an improved acetate fabric that doesn't melt as easily and is easier to care for.

ACRYLIC is a fine, soft, luxurious fabric with the bulk and hand (or feel) of wool. Lightweight and springy, this fabric is non-allergenic, dries quickly, draws moisture away from the body and is washable. Acrylic does not take even a moderate amount of heat. Modacrylics are used in pile fabrics like fake fur and are more flame-resistant.

LASTEX is an elastic fibre made from latex. It is most often used with other fibres to create fabrics such as spandex and foundation garments. Lastex will deteriorate after repeated washing and drying, gradually losing its elasticity.

Man Made fabric.

NYLON is stronger yet weighs less than any other commonly used fibre. It is elastic and resilient and responsive to heat-setting. Nylon fibres are smooth and non-absorbent, and dry quickly. Dirt doesn't cling to this smooth fibre, nor is it weakened by chemicals or perspiration. Extensive washing and drying in an automatic dryer can eventually cause piling. Nylon whites should be washed separately to avoid greying. This fabric may yellow, so it should be bleached frequently with sodium perborate bleach. Nylon melts at high temperatures. If ironing is necessary, always use a low temperature on the wrong side.

POLYESTER is a strong fibre that is resistant to creasing and thus keeps its shape. Polyester melts at medium to high temperatures. Blends of polyester give cotton a permanent press property and extend the wear of these blended garments. Threads spun from polyester fibres are strong, wear exceptionally well, and are used extensively in home sewing and manufactured sewing.

RAYON, from cellulose, has many of the qualities of cotton. Rayon is strong, extremely absorbent, comes in a variety of qualities and weights, and can be made to resemble natural fabrics. Rayon does not melt but burns at high temperatures. It drapes well, has a soft, silky hand, and a smooth, napped (or bulky) surface. Rayon will wrinkle easily and may stretch when wet and shrink when washed.

SPANDEX is an elastic-type fibre that can be stretched many times its length and still springs back to the original length. Spandex is more resistant than latex to washing, perspiration and heat. Spandex is used in foundation garments and hosiery.

Wool fabric comes in many forms.

FAB
RIC
ID

—

Junky Styling promote an addiction to recycling and a need for individualism.

the properties of natural fabrics

NATURAL FABRICS are created from the fibres of the coats of animals, silkworm cocoons, the seeds of plants, and leaves and stems.

WOOL fabric brings to mind cosy warmth. Some wools are scratchy, giving some people the idea that they are 'allergic' to wool. Although wool fibre comes from a variety of animal coats, not all wools are scratchy, and many are extremely soft. When wool is washed at too high a temperature, it shrinks and turns into felt. Wool will not only return to its original position after being stretched or creased, it will absorb up to 30% of its weight in moisture without feeling damp. Its unique properties allow shaping and tailoring, making wool the most popular fabric for tailoring fine garments. Wool is also dirt-resistant, flame-resistant and, in many weaves, resists wear and tearing.

COTTON, cool, soft and comfortable, is the principal clothing fibre of the world. Cotton 'breathes'. It can stand high temperatures and takes dyes easily. Chlorine bleach can be used to restore white cotton garments to a clear white but this bleach may yellow chemically finished cottons or remove colour in dyed cottons. Boiling and sterilising temperatures can also be used on cotton without it disintegrating. Cotton can also be ironed at relatively high temperatures, stands up to abrasion and wears well. It is often blended with other fibres such as polyester, linen and wool, so as to obtain the best properties of each fibre.

SILK and silk garments are prized for their versatility, wearability and comfort. Silk is the strongest natural fibre. A steel filament of the same diameter as silk will break before a filament of silk does. Silk absorbs moisture, which makes it cool in the summer and warm in the winter. Because of its high absorbency, it is easily dyed in many deep colours. Silk retains its shape, drapes well, caresses the figure, and shimmers. It's elegant, versatile and washable.

Silk is a natural protein fibre, like human hair, taken from the cocoon of the silkworm. The natural glue, sericin, secreted by silkworms and not totally removed during the manufacturing of the silk, is a natural sizing agent, which is brought out when washing the fabric in warm water. Most silk fabrics can be hand-washed. Technically, unlike other fibres silk does not shrink, though if the fabric is not tightly woven, washing a silk will tighten up the weave. Silk garments, moreover, can shrink if the fabric has not been washed prior to garment construction. When washing silk, do not wring, but roll it in a towel. Silk dries quickly but should not be put in an automatic dryer unless the fabric has been dried in a similar dryer prior to garment construction. A good shampoo works well on silk. It will remove oil and revitalise the fabric. Do not use an alkaline shampoo or one which contains ingredients such as wax, petroleum or their derivatives, as these products will leave a residue on your silk and may cause 'oil' spots. If static or clinging is a problem with your silks, a good hair conditioner may be used in the rinse water. Silk may yellow and fade with the use of a high iron setting. Press cloths and a steam iron are recommended. Silk is also weakened by sunlight and perspiration.

LINEN is elegant, beautiful and durable, the refined luxury fabric. Linen is the strongest of the vegetable fibres and has 2 to 3 times the strength of cotton. Not only is the linen fibre strong, it is also smooth, making the finished fabric lint-free. Even better, linen only gets softer and finer the more it is washed. Creamy white to light tan, this fibre can be easily dyed and the colour does not fade when washed. Linen does wrinkle easily but also presses easily. Linen, like cotton, can also be boiled without damaging the fibre. Highly absorbent and a good conductor of heat, this fabric is cool in garments. However, constant creasing in the same place in sharp folds will tend to break the linen threads. This wear can show up in collars and hems, and in any area that is iron creased during the laundering. Linen has poor elasticity and does not spring back readily.

HEMP fabric is like linen in both hand and appearance. Hemp fabric withstands water better than any other textile product. It wrinkles easily and should not be creased excessively, to avoid wear and breakage of the fibres.

wardrobe surgery

Junky has built a reputation over the last ten years not only for our tailored detail-rich fresh styles, but also for encouraging the customers to get involved in recycling.

'Wardrobe surgery' is the service that allows customers to bring their old/worn out/tragic garments to the Junky store and be part of the redesign process by explaining why they haven't thrown the offending article away and what they'd like it turned into. Some customers request recreations of the shopfloor styles to be made from their own clothes or inherited garments, but others commission wedding dresses and red-carpet creations. No garment construction is beyond the talents of the Junky team.

Every project differs in the amount of time and complexity involved, so customers are quoted a price after a consultation.

WARDROBE SURGERY PROCEDURE

When a customer brings in an item for wardrobe surgery we always have a discussion to determine what they require or desire. Most things are achievable, so the next step is to work out how much they want to spend and if there's a deadline. Every request is individual: even if there are hundreds of ill-fitting jackets rocking around, every customer wants to wear their 'Junkyfied' one in a different way.

OUR COMMITMENT TO OUR CUSTOMERS

Right from the start, we have always designed for our customers. We embrace their individuality and discerning tastes. We were our first customers, and then we quickly focused on anyone who was into our label. Responding to needs and demands has shaped our clothing collection and retail offer. We enjoy listening to feedback on the designs and 'tweaking' garments to give a made-to-measure feel. This approach has ensured a loyal following and enables us to make garments with real people in mind.

Emily and Chris in dressed Junky favourites.

customer profiles

CHRIS RICHMOND VIDEO DIRECTOR & FILM-MAKER

WHY DO YOU LIKE JUNKY?

I choose clothes on the basis of their originality and design, and I chose Junky because they are timeless clothes that reflect my personality. I'm not a show-off (I'm actually quite shy) but I enjoy the comments that I get when I am wearing Junky clothing. It's important to me that I buy a piece of clothing that is exclusive to me. I like the fact they produce one-off pieces.

Through Worldwide Wardrobe Surgery we want to change the way people consume clothing.

Ness Sherry, photographer.

YOUR FAVOURITE JUNKY PIECE?

It is a three-piece, tailor-made suit creation, made for a friend's wedding. It's a vintage Pierre Cardin suit reworked with denim. The fabric is a woven suiting that's a grey/black/greeny tone, and the denim is dark but faded. The trousers are mid-calf length and have large denim knee pockets and a denim wraparound skirt section at the hips. When worn as a three-piece, these are the focal point of the suit. The waistcoat is high buttoning with denim detail and the jacket fitted me perfectly and had subtle denim and structure details.

The reason this ensemble became my favourite is because each piece worked so well on its own and went on to make striking outfits. The jacket unfortunately was stolen in California, an incident that my wardrobe has never quite recovered from, but the waistcoat has become a great staple of my look.

EMILY CHALMERS
AUTHOR AND OWNER OF CARAVAN BOUTIQUE

WHY DO YOU LIKE JUNKY?

I've always found Junky inspiring. I like the mix of modern design using old classics, and the result of that combination is an original and interesting mix. I particularly like the way that they use shirting and suit fabrics.

YOUR FAVOURITE JUNKY PIECE?

Well, my favourite piece was a wrist cuff made from charcoal suiting with a pink and black-spotted silk trim. I took this off to wash up somewhere and have never seen it since. This was without doubt my most worn piece.

Another favourite would be my husband's tie-bottomed, silver-grey trousers. He only wore them for special occasions and I decided they needed to get out more. A very quick button addition converted them to fit me and creates a fold on the front that complements the design. Now I wear them all the time.

NESS SHERRY, PHOTOGRAPHER

WHAT DOES JUNKY STYLING MEAN TO YOU?

To me Junky Styling represents innovative designs that make me look and feel great. It's quite amazing because when I put on my favourite jacket it's like donning a confidence cloak! It says exactly what I want it to say about me – I'm different, original, and you can't label me.

YOUR FAVOURITE JUNKY PIECE?

My structured jacket is my all-time favourite. It is navy blue with a faint pinstripe and has a red zip for a splash of colour. It fits me like a glove and I always get compliments whenever I wear it.

NATHAN WOODHEAD, PROJECT MANAGER

WHY DO YOU LIKE JUNKY STYLING?

I think of myself as an urban dandy and I like to be noticed. I think they make some really cool stuff and it slips into my existing wardrobe (built up over years) really well. People always ask me where did I get my Junky pieces from, and, as much as I hate telling them, I love the fact that I get clocked for looking different.

YOUR FAVOURITE JUNKY PIECE?

I love my waistcoat. I knew I needed a new waistcoat but never dreamed I'd find one as good as this. The sections of different fabric, pockets and button tabs all float my boat, but the most important thing is the fit – it fits me so well. It also goes with a multitude of different looks like with my Baker-Boy trousers rolled up and a smart pair of shoes, or my skinny jeans and a shirt. I could even team it with smart grey trousers and wear it to a wedding.

KURT WILLIAMS, ACTOR & JEWELLERY DESIGNER

WHY JUNKY?

I shop at Junky because they have fierce styles and they are constantly coming up with new designs that I love. They should give me their clothes for free because I wear them well and always testify (to anyone who wants to know) about how amazing they are! On a more serious note, I really respect the way they promote being original and individual – they ensure that every garment is in some way unique to the owner. I also respect the way the garments are carefully constructed with beautiful finishing touches and details. They have their own signature on style and it complements mine perfectly.

YOUR MOST LOVED JUNKY PIECE?

Check out the beautiful collar on this jacket – it's made from the sleeves of some other jacket. The way it fastens down the front is gorgeous and really different. Despite all the little features and crazy details, this jacket looks quite classic and elegant. I wear this particular piece when I'm feeling a bit resigned or subdued so people can focus more on the jacket and less on me.

Nathan posing in his waistcoat.

Kurt working the Junky look.

Jimmy on the shop sofa after purchasing his jacket.

Jody Williams.

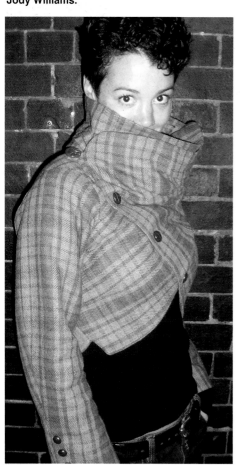

JIMMY K-TEL, DJ, EVENTS & PROMOTION

WHY DO YOU LIKE JUNKY?

The thing with Junky is that it's like my name is already sewn into the back of every new piece I buy. It's more than just a piece of clothing – it's a new friend that I will have adventures with! Not only does it reflect and enhance my personality, it has an identity of its own. It's more than clothing, it's a feeling – it makes you feel confident not arrogant … no, actually, it does make me feel a tiny bit arrogant...!!!

YOUR BEST JUNKY PIECE?

At the moment it's my checked brown bomber jacket. It's been fashioned from a shirt and is the perfect weight for a summer evening. It's got a wicked casual shape and a nice fit. I feel like I'm dressed well without trying – effortless. It's the close attention to detail that really does it for me, like the way they've laid the buttons and buttonhole strips across the shoulders and down the front – quite unnecessary but super-subtle styling.

JODY WILLIAMS, MAKE-UP ARTIST & STYLIST

WHY JUNKY?

Junky for me represents the ultimate, inspirational form of bespoke styling at its best.

YOUR FAVOURITE JUNKY PIECE?

It would be a cliché to say 'there are too many to choose from', because everything I try on and have to buy is precious, but my flavour of the month and most currently worn garment is my green army-knit jumper/dress, but I'm torn between this and my plaid high-neck wool jacket because I'm always looking for a reason to wear it. I only wear one piece at a time because I wouldn't want any piece to detract from another. Each item deserves its own appreciation and respect. I suppose I regard them as pieces of art.

conclusion

PREVIOUS PAGE Styled
by Io Takemura. Hair by
Tomi. Make up by Carol
Brown. Photo by Syk.

The future of fashion lies in inspiring not dictating.

Junky Styling has developed
a solid identity over the last
decade. We represent a fusion
of original, timeless British design
and strong ethics. This suits us just fine,
because when we set out recycling old
clothes, it was never an intention to build
a pioneering concept brand; we were just happy being creative, looking
good and earning just enough money to call it a business.

Our belief in the importance of recycling clothes into wearable,
sustainable fashions has always been the foundation of our business. This
belief has been backed up with daring, brilliant designs. Now, 10 years on,
I can bring myself to 'give it the large' and big up our concept and work,
though, of course, with anything creative, or style- or art-based, 'one man's
junk is another man's treasure'. We've always been of the mentality that it's
down to others to rate what we do or pay the compliments – not believing
the hype or being up our own arses is the way we are.

'Sustainable fashion' is a fairly new buzz term, one that gets applied to
Junky Styling, but the two words seem to contradict each other in meaning.
We are all about investing in our clothing and wardrobes. We want every
fashion consumer to look at garments in a different way – to see the
recyclable potential, the quality of cloth and durability of design.

Not to be on any high horses, or part of the 'greener than thou' brigade,
but we are very passionate about safeguarding the earth's resources.
It's essential to the future of everything – which nowadays is no longer
profound wisdom, just plain common sense. Junky Styling demonstrates

that even within the disposable, fickle world of fashion, it is still possible to exercise ecological awareness.

Other fashion labels have to be commercial, and retailers are bound by overheads and lack of money. This restricts their ability to put sensible ideology into practice using environmentally sound products. We, on the other hand, are only bound by fair-trading ethics, and enjoy the freedom our in-house production gives us. We enable people to make considered choices about how they want to shop. The drive towards sustainable practices in fashion is all about the consumer. When we look at the increase in awareness and sales for 'organic' produce, we feel that a shift is well underway and that consumers have come to care as much about what they wear on their bodies as what they put in them.

This changing consumer perception has been essential to our success. We are appreciated because our work has a timelessness to it that makes it transcend fashion and become clothing that one keeps returning to again and again. What's even better, once you've had enough of it, it can always be recycled into something else. This flexibility has kept us progressing, and we have made some big waves for such a small company. The recognition we get leaves us no other option than to expand, as the issues that we are facing are bigger than all of us. Junky Styling's ideas and concepts are having a global effect.

We plan to set up 'wardrobe-surgery salons' in every major city across the world. People would be able to walk into these shops, pick a stylist and discuss then instruct design work on their treasured or out-of-date items of clothing. This facility would turn every clothing purchase into an investment, and the bespoke nature of the service would ensure individuality.

FACING PAGES The crew: David, Eric, Anni and Kerry at the end of many catwalk events – exhausted yet ecstatic!

CON
CLU
SION

The shops would be set up a bit like hairdressing salons, with several designers, each specialising in different areas of garment reconstruction. This would provide very much-needed employment to fashion designers, seamstresses, pattern-cutters and especially graduates (90% of fashion graduates never get to work in the fashion industry). Portfolios and client lists could be built in these environments and the experience would almost certainly lead to bigger and better things – making room for other employees to come in.

We have identified that a 'recycling academy' is needed, as there is nowhere that teaches how to deconstruct and reconstruct in a professional capacity, and we would be the perfect company to set this up. It is very important to pass on our skills and inspire people to learn how to use up 'fashion waste'.

We are also looking to develop franchised versions of the Junky Styling store. This decision came about as a direct result of designers in other countries such as the USA and Dubai getting in touch and asking if they could set up a shop like ours with our products and support. It seems there are many places in the world in desperate need of different, original and inspiring fashion.

All in all, we have a long road to travel to take our work to the levels we intend. The future will be challenging and varied, but best of all, the future is creative and bright.

the show is over!

THE EXTREMELY INCONVENIENT ADVENTURES of Bronte Mettlestone

GUPPY
BOOKS

THE EXTREMELY INCONVENIENT
ADVENTURES OF BRONTE METTLESTONE
is a GUPPY BOOK

First published in the UK in 2019
by Guppy Books,
Bracken Hill,
Cotswold Road,
Oxford OX2 9JG

This edition published in 2020

First published in Australia by Allen and Unwin in 2017

Text copyright © Jaclyn Moriarty
Illustrations copyright © Karl James Mountford

978 1 913101 05 3

1 3 5 7 9 10 8 6 4 2

Papers used by Guppy Books are from well-managed
forests and other responsible sources.

MIX
Paper from
responsible sources
FSC® C020471

GUPPY PUBLISHING LTD Reg. No. 11565833

A CIP catalogue record for this book is available from the British Library.

Printed and bound in Great Britain by CPI Books Ltd